SPIRITS OF THE SAND

SPIRITS OF THE SAND

Richard T Bass

MENIN HOUSE

Also by Richard T Bass

Spirits of the Sand – field edition (2005)
Precious Cargo (1993)
The Brigades of Neptune (1994)
Clear the Way (1996)
Exercise Tiger (2012)

For more information please visit www.exercise-tiger.com

Menin House an imprint of
Tommies Guides Military Booksellers & Publishers
Gemini House
136-140 Old Shoreham Road
Brighton
BN3 7BD
www.tommiesguides.co.uk

This edition published in Great Britain by
Menin House Publishers 2014

A catalogue record for this book is available from the British Library

ISBN 978-1-908336-66-8

Cover design by Ryan Gearing

CONTENTS

CHAPTER ONE

THE U.S. Assault Training Centre was a truly unique establishment. It was the only one of its kind in wartime Great Britain where American soldiers learned, trained and practised newly developed amphibious assault tactics to lead the assault across the beaches of Normandy on D-Day, 6th June 1944.

In 1943 its formation came about through sheer necessity, following an unforgivable oversight at the very highest level of American war planning which had assumed troops destined to lead the invasion of Europe would arrive in Britain already trained for their task. Realisation this was not the case created a tense situation that had to be urgently rectified as the date for the invasion of Europe was only a few months ahead.

Great Britain's declaration of war with Germany in September 1939 and America's hasty declaration of neutrality was followed by two years of agonising political debate in the United States. President Roosevelt believed his nation would eventually become embroiled in the European conflict and promoted support for Great Britain but in opposition were "Isolationists" who with some justification took the view that the squabble in Europe had nothing to do with them, harking back to the 126,000 American soldiers killed during the First World War when the United States had tipped the balance of power, and victory, in England's favour.

The Japanese attack on Pearl Harbour on 7th December 1941 changed this division of opinion into a united determination and common purpose. Whether or not the Japanese declaration of war upon the United States was actually received prior to the Japanese attack is open to debate but it was the climax of year-long "tit for tat" commercial and diplomatic actions. The predicted and immediate reflex action was the declaration of war upon Japan by the United States and the British Empire followed a few days later by Germany and Italy declaring war on the United States in support of their Japanese ally.

The American nation quickly mobilised their war industries and expanded their armed forces, catapulting the United States army of just over a quarter of a million men from 15th place in world armies' ranking to over eight million men at arms by 1944. Nearly 18 million young men were drafted; 10 million were accepted for military service and those destined for the army undertook the "Army General Classification Test", a 40 minute test of vocabulary and arithmetic enabling the army to assess their most appropriate trade, skills and promotion prospects. The majority went to the newly mobilised seventy three infantry divisions to spend an average of 16 months overseas. Thousands of young men set out on what they saw as a grand adventure across the Atlantic blissfully unaware of the horrors that lay before them and their military master's immense problem of training them.

In 1943 no principle existed within the U.S. Army for assaulting a heavily fortified and defensively prepared coastline, and the only published advice in a U.S. Army Field Manual was ... "*Fortified areas are avoided in the initial assault and taken from the rear* ... ". Colonel Chase the Assault Training Centre's Chief of training later remarked "*nice work if you can get it*". Therefore assaulting the enemy held coastline of Normandy required not only the creation of a new and unique doctrine but also the training of thousands of troops in those principles, and time was short. British and Canadian troops were already well advanced in their training programmes and Allied war planners were steadily evolving logistical solutions for the greatest amphibious assault in military history, except American troops weren't ready.

This lack of readiness and need for specialised training was emphasised in a July 1943 study of the ATC. "*American divisions earmarked for the assault phase of the invasion will, in general, have been trained in landing assault operations prior to arrival in the U.K. This pre-training in the U.S., however, will have been conducted under conditions of tide, surf and beach which are dissimilar to the conditions to be encountered in Europe. It follows that there exists a real need for facilities designed to adapt the basic doctrines as practised in the U.S. training centers to the specific requirements of the forthcoming invasion*".

The American high command acknowledged this and had to select an individual with the right qualifications, experience and personality who could head up this task. Combing personnel files the name of Lieutenant Colonel Paul W. Thompson stood out. He was a career engineer soldier, graduating from West Point in 1929, and had spent 1935 to 1937 in Nazi Germany as a military attaché to the United States embassy in Berlin where he had spent a period of attachment with the German 16th Engineer Battalion learning their theory and practice of defensive fortifications. Described by General John C.H. Lee, commanding Service of Supplies, ETO as "*our best informed officer on German technique, organization and tactics*". Colonel Lyle C. Metheny the Assault Training Centre's Executive Officer stated that Thompson was … "*appointed to commanding officer by direction of the President*".

Thompson was kicking his heels behind a military desk in the Intelligence branch, Office of the Chief Engineer in Washington D.C., frustrated at the prospect of the war passing him by with no opportunity to see action, so eagerly accepted the appointment to create and run an assault training centre. Arriving in England in January 1943 he discovered that "*the Assault Training Centre turned out to be little more than a gleam in the eye of the Theater G-3 (Operations section)*". He was confirmed in his title as Commandant of the Assault Training Centre, which was activated on 2nd April 1943 and at that stage existed only on paper, but by the end of April 1943 after considerable work in thrashing out just what was expected of him, his mission was finally committed to paper by the European Theatre of Operations headquarters on 6th May 1943 coinciding with Thompson's promotion to full Colonel.

Hindering his task of getting down to details was the difference of basic strategy between the Americans and the British. The Americans strongly favoured the most direct route to the black heart of Nazi Germany, a brash straight line knockout punch that would involve invasion forces crossing the narrow Dover Straits to assault the Calais area. Acknowledged by them as the most strongly defended part of the whole French coast and anticipated by the Germans as being the Allies most likely choice of invasion coastline, the British disagreed.

Their view was based upon logistical practicality dictating that Normandy should be the invasion area for several very good reasons. Normandy was directly opposite Portsmouth and Southampton across the English Channel and these were the only central southern ports of England capable of handling the quantities of shipping envisaged. This was supported by their 1941 estimate that 2,250 landing craft would be required for the invasion in addition to other shipping. Their argument continued that smaller ports to east and west of Portsmouth and Southampton would provide additional accommodation for shipping of the vast invasion armada. Considering the expected fanatical German defence from long prepared positions of strength no matter where they landed on the French coastline, Normandy attracted favour with the British as defences there were only partially completed by comparison with those in the Pas de Calais. Additionally, the entire Normandy hinterland could be easily isolated simply by destroying bridges over the rivers Seine and Loire, effectively blocking German reinforcements from reaching Normandy. Intelligence suggested there were no German units of sufficient calibre or strength near the anticipated beachhead to mount a major counter attack and Normandy was within easy range of air support from Britain. The British rounded off their arguments by declaring the Cherbourg peninsula was capable of affording some protection for the Normandy invasion anchorages from the prevailing Atlantic weather whereas the Dover Straits were too restrictive and shallow for shipping manoeuvres, and much too far from the south west ports to send an American force, undetected, up the English Channel to Calais. The matter was debated at great length and eventually resolved in favour of Normandy, so Colonel Thompson now knew what defences he had to overcome, and with an invasion target date of May 1944 he now had the basis of a timetable.

Thompson's mission was two-fold. Firstly, to produce a doctrine for assaulting a heavily defended enemy coastline and establish a beachhead, and having done that from scratch, he then had to train combat troops in those principles.

To clarify his mission and gain authority for what he considered necessary to accomplish it Thompson had early pressed for confirmation which was duly granted and formalised in a memorandum of 6th May 1943 from Major General Key, Adjutant General of the U.S. Army. The Assault Training Centre was principally to ..."*develop and keep up to date the doctrine and methods covering the assault of enemy held coasts, particularly of Western Europe...to prepare and operate the Assault Training Center for the reception and training of such organizations as may be selected for this type of training*".

General Key insisted plans for the Assault Training Centre to accomplish this should be submitted for approval without delay, so as Commandant of the only American establishment tasked with training soldiers for the anticipated invasion of Europe, he soon realised that the very success or failure of the American D-Day landings lay fully upon his shoulders.

CHAPTER TWO

THE Assault Training Centre's assault doctrine was developed by a conference Thompson convened on 23rd May 1943 to run for a whole month. Military experts were seconded from every Allied service to thrash out a workable method for the Americans to neutralise German defences on their assigned beaches in Normandy. Ordered by Thompson and organised by Colonel Lucius P. Chase the conference called on speakers from experimental projects, Allied navy and air forces and intelligence sources. The conference amassed vast amounts of data and photographs to be analysed, and drew upon the combat experience of commanders of similar amphibious landings, including the raid on Dieppe. The British regarded this as a disaster whereas the Americans believed it to be a partial success because "*at least the tanks got ashore*". The Dieppe raid commander Major General Roberts conceded the Canadians had got nearly all their tanks ashore but lost most of them when they tried to cross the sea wall to enter the town. Another Dieppe experience that heavily influenced the conference conclusions was that naval guns had made little impression on concrete emplacements.

The American problem was how to overcome a "heavily defended coastline", defined at the conference by Colonel Burton of British Intelligence as "*the closeness of one strongpoint to another. In a more heavily defended area they will be 1,000 yards apart; in a less defended area they will be two to three thousand yards apart*".

Thompson knew other establishments were already involved in researching and developing amphibious assaults which could be useful to his doctrine conference. The U.S. Army Amphibian

Command at Camp Edwards, Massachusetts was concerned with shore to shore operations. Army Ground Forces Amphibious Command at Carabelle, Florida, was developing its own amphibious assault tactics and also ran a two week "Engineer School course" at Fort Belvoir, Virginia, but as Thompson discovered, their tactics were based purely upon theory with no full scale exercises, thereby rendering their doctrine "*possibly unsound*". General McNair had increased divisional training in the United States by one week to include combined operations, generally following the AGF "Engineer School course" principles. The U.S. Navy and Marine Corps were co-operating in developing tactics using their recent experiences in the Pacific theatre of operations but problems there were quite different to those in Europe. The British, Thompson estimated, were ahead in many aspects of developing assault techniques due to their greater practical experience and concluded that despite these agencies independently developing amphibious assault operations, there was no co-ordination or liaison to produce a firm doctrine and he had to develop his own.

Thompson's conference delegates considered every aspect of the problem, especially the terrain and topography to be encountered on the Normandy beaches selected for the American assault. This was probably the most crucial element that dictated the whole doctrine, for unlike the British and Canadian assaults destined to cross sandy beaches onto undulating grass lands, the Americans would be faced with steep bluffs and only a few narrow valleys leading off the beach to the plateau above "Omaha". "Utah" beach had different problems of topography with a low dune line behind the beach and then a vast area of flooded farm land with only four causeways across it compelling invading forces to concentrate on securing and using those causeways to take the fight inland. So while the British and Canadians could immediately use their tanks, the Americans had to seize the valleys and causeways leading off their beaches, leaving them no alternative but to attack the defences with infantry, and land their tanks once access off the beach had been secured.

An early conference view was that initial objectives should not be too ambitious given the lack of large calibre firepower that could be landed in the first waves and uncertain success of naval and aerial bombardment. This cautious view was later confirmed by Colonel Horton when he reported to Thompson on 3rd December 1943 that he had observed a recent brigade landing exercise involving the 3rd Canadian Division. He pointed out the usual differences in the British approach to the problem – using Royal Engineer assault tanks ahead of assault infantry and use of engineer tanks soon after – and he especially noted from this exercise that the depth of initial objectives were becoming less and less, approaching more closely to the American conception.

The new doctrine was slowly being shaped not only by terrain characteristics restricting the conventional use of armour and infantry but also by a universal lack of large landing craft. Providentially there was an available surplus of the humble LCVP, a thirty man capacity craft which proved to be the mainstay of the doctrine that was taking shape. This was in accord with the conference conclusion that … *"the outcome of the final assault on beach defences will depend on small unit leadership and thorough training and determination of individual soldiers and small groups to a much larger extent than is normally the case"*. The idea of creating "assault type" divisions or regiments had been early discarded as too cumbersome and time consuming to convert from existing units, so thirty-man "Infantry Assault Teams" were created from within those same divisions. To achieve this, regimental companies were simply re-organised from 6 officers and 198 enlisted men into "Assault Companies" containing six "Infantry Assault Teams", each of 1 officer and 29 men. Therefore three "Assault Companies" still made one battalion, a unit still recognisable as part of a division. Approval for this restructuring of conventional army units was sought from the highest quarter and approved only a few days later.

Unit commanders had to be convinced about this re-organisation and one of the first problems encountered by ATC training staff was selling the idea to them as this deviated from familiar tactics and techniques, and introduced the novelty of amphibious landings. This was an issue that required diplomacy and rank to convince sceptical commanders that this was the way things had to be done, and the task

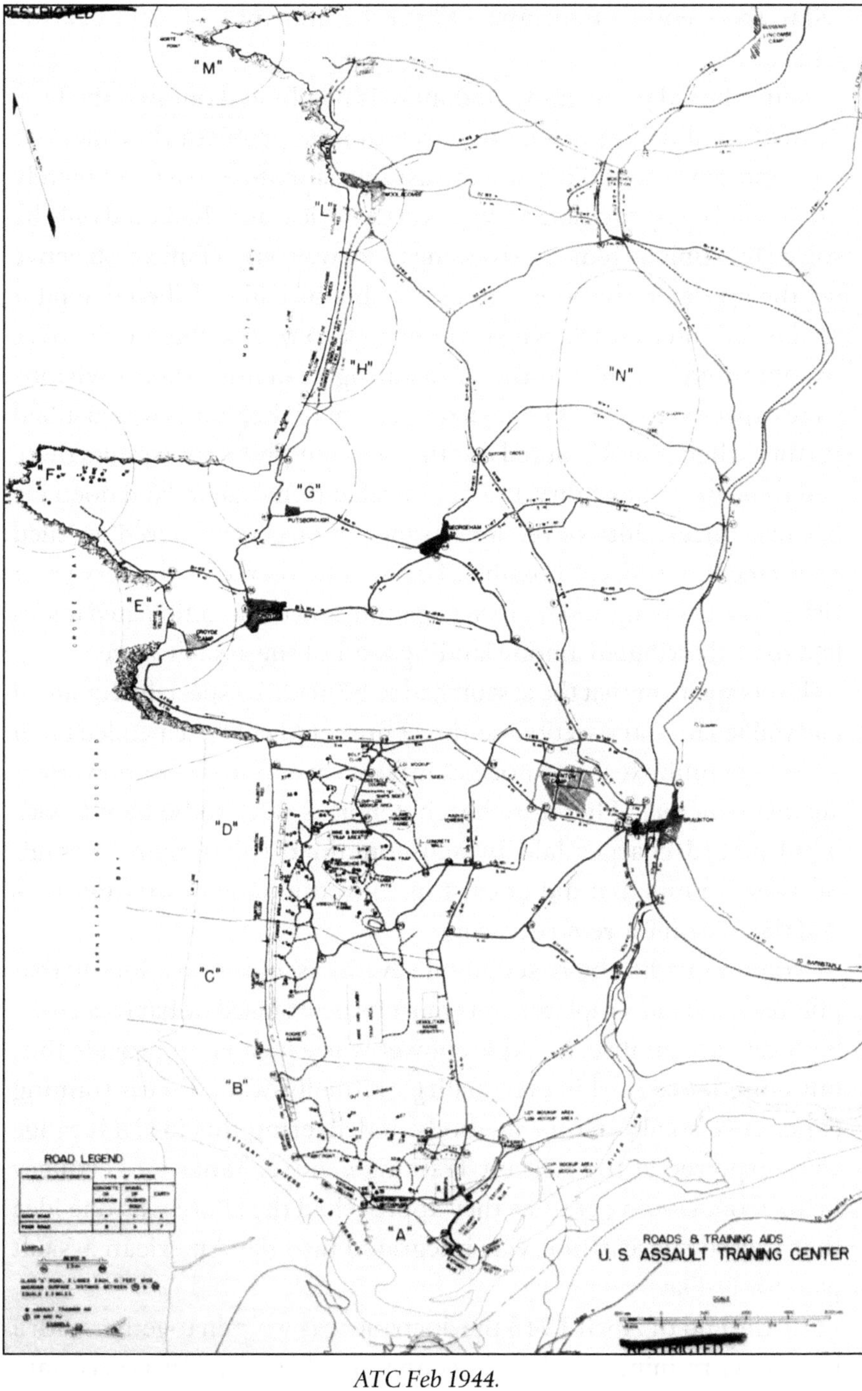
"M"
"L"
"H"
"N"
"F"
"G"
PUTSBOROUGH
GEORGEHAM
"E"
"D"
BRAUNTON
"C"
"B"
"A"
ROAD LEGEND
ROADS & TRAINING AIDS
U. S. ASSAULT TRAINING CENTER

ATC Feb 1944.

fell to the Centre's Executive Officer, Lieutenant Colonel Lucius P. Chase.

With the aid of diagrams and models he pointed out that the U.S. Army found itself presented with a unique problem they had not encountered before. They were to assault a fortified coast, not merely a defended coast such as Sicily or North Africa, and this could only be solved by a unique remedy, stressing there was only a limited objective for their assault divisions – to establish a beachhead then defend it against counter-attack. Most were quick to realise these objectives were limited because of the devastating casualties their divisions were expected to bear. The re-arrangement of their units was justified further when it was pointed out that with amphibious assaults there had to be more flexibility and decentralization than in land doctrine because uncertainty of reconnaissance of targets rendered detailed assignment of tasks impossible. This was furthered by the very great risk of craft sinking and faulty navigation, and these anticipated losses had to be distributed among landing craft of the assault waves.

It was spelt out that the assault had to be made by specially equipped and trained infantry sections as direct fire could not be depended upon to reduce pillboxes, and normal infantry weapons were powerless against concrete. Therefore beach defences were to be blown with hand placed charges laid by self-contained thirty-man "Assault Sections", units that didn't exist in conventional infantry divisions and the reason for re-structuring.

Training had to be based upon several assumptions. Firstly that pillboxes and gun emplacements must be neutralised by flat trajectory, high velocity gunfire. Naval firepower was expected to provide this, but confidence in this eventuality gradually waned with training experience so alternative methods of delivering this initial barrage were explored at the Assault Training Centre. Tanks and artillery firing from landing craft as they approached the shore was one idea that was so successful it was integrated into the American assault plan for D-Day.

By the end of April 1943 the doctrine was written together with a three week training schedule the conference determined was necessary to adequately train soldiers in these new tactics. It still required refinement but a secret document of the time gives an appreciation of the problem and the broad American solution … *"Modern fortified areas are characterized by a series of steel pillboxes, steel turrets, open emplacements, troop shelters, slit trenches and similar installations. Such defences are commonly called Hedgehog.*

The heart of the defensive system is the concrete and steel pillboxes. These are camouflaged, project only a small portion above the ground, and are so located as to provide interlocking zones of fire and mutual fire support. The entire area is surrounded by various anti-tank obstacles, ditches, tank traps, minefields, and from two to many bands of wire. The wire, minefields and normal avenues of approach for foot troops are liberally sewn with anti-personnel mines. The ground immediately before the weapon openings, or embrasures, in the pillboxes is levelled to provide long fields of fire. Where natural cover in the form of trees or underbrush is present, the trees and brush are cut down. Generally little, if any, natural cover for attacking troops exists.

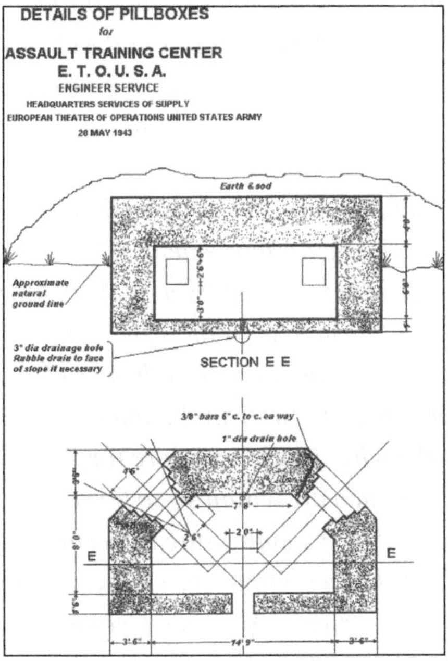

Pillbox Early Type.

The pillboxes have weapons that vary from machine guns to anti-tank guns up to light field artillery.

To successfully attack such a formidable area of new construction embodying the latest principles of modern tactics, infantry must be specifically trained, provided with additional weapons, and be backed up with a preponderance of artillery and direct fire weapons. In addition, air bombardment and ground support formations are extensively employed".

The technique for direct assault of such hedgehog fortifications to be taught at the Assault Training Centre followed a general plan

...*"Infantry to be reorganized into assault sections; with flamethrowers and high explosive teams being the heart of the assault section. The troops advance under massed artillery and direct fire weapons preceded by an aerial bombardment, and covered by smoke. However, no reliance is placed upon actually reducing pillboxes by action other than direct assault.*

The air and ground bombardments are relied upon to crater the area, spoiling the fields of fire and providing some cover, knock out the enemy artillery, destroy some of the open emplacements, and to cause the pillboxes to "button-up", thereby allowing the infantry assault sections to advance and close with the enemy.

Upon the close approach of the assault troops, the artillery lifts to the rear areas, preventing the enemy bringing up reinforcements. The direct fire weapons, normally anti-tank guns, tanks, tank destroyers and infantry cannon continue to fire directly on the embrasures until their fire is masked by the infantry. At this point the assault troops cover the advance of the flamethrowers and demolition teams with rifle, anti-tank, and bazooka fire. Wire cutting teams cut or blow the wire using Bangalore torpedoes. When the flamethrower and demolition men are within 40 to 60 yards of the embrasures, the flamethrower is fired at the embrasure to permit the demolition men to place their high explosives within the embrasure. In short, the demolition team are the "ball carriers". All other weapons and men are used to permit the demolition men to place their charges, thereby accomplishing the job of knocking out the pillbox.

Engineer troops closely follow the assault sections, and clear gaps thru the minefields, bridge anti-tank ditches and other tank obstacles to facilitate the forward movement of the track and wheeled vehicles. In most cases, Hedgehog are echeloned in depth. In other words there are successive bands of these positions, several hundred yards apart in depth depending upon the terrain".

The London conference was formally closed on 23rd June 1943 by Brigadier General Daniel Noce, Assistant Chief of Staff, G-3, ETOUSA who said ..."*The Assault Training Center is approved. We will have an important mission to perform in our work here*". Colonel Thompson added ..."*the conference would get us off to a flying start, and (we) think that some day it will pay off on the beaches*".

Once the doctrine had been finalised, principles of training were addressed. An Assault Training Centre resident "School Battalion" was created from various sections of the 156th Infantry Regiment totalling 125 officers and warrant officers and 2,607 enlisted men. They tested the training programme for a month at Woolacombe when it was found that only a few minor alterations were necessary to individual lesson plans so the Assault Training Centre was ready for its first trainees. Colonel Myles W. Brewster recorded that the first combat troops to attend the ATC were the cadre of the 29th Infantry Division that trained for ten days prior to the arrival of their Regimental Combat Team. "*Then under supervision of ATC personnel, this cadre trained the RCT. While the 1st RCT was being trained, the cadre of the 2nd RCT was trained. It, in turn, trained the second RCT. This was the procedure of training of all RCTs. The cadre of an RCT would train with the current RCT, then train its own RCT*".

Amphibious assaults required the closest co-operation of the U.S. Navy and they were approached at the earliest opportunity to participate in planning. Across the estuary, opposite the army site were established, small British naval bases at Appledore and Instow which appeared to the army to adequately meet the navy's anticipated needs, but the navy thought otherwise and were almost obstructive in taking them over. This reluctance to assist and support the army continued for some months until the commanding officer was changed. Navy landing craft crews eventually took advantage of army activities and ran their own training courses of between two and four weeks depending upon the army's requirements and the weather. Crews at Appledore were rotated with others from St. Mawes and Falmouth in Cornwall until late December 1943 when the Cornish bases started their own exercises. At the height of activity the U.S. Navy had 60 LCVPs, 16 LCMs and 7 LCTs at Appledore and Instow with a complement of 60 officers and 700 men.

The mission of the U.S. Assault Training Centre was written by Thompson and summarised in a "Secret" letter dated 12th July 1943 which set out each assault division's mission, their training requirements, and the Assault Training Centre's responsibilities.

One example for Assault & Support Companies simplistically shows their operational mission as " *Land from LCVPs, assault and reduce beach fortifications, pass wire and minefields, help organise a beachhead line and defeat counter attack*". It was deduced from the mission that their training should include " *proper methods of embarking in, debarking from, and wading ashore from landing craft; acquire individual skill in use of assault weapons; develop co-ordination of weapons in the assault; learn use of local smoke; methods of passing minefields and booby traps, and methods of crossing wire; develop fire and movement teamwork by an Assault Section in the assault of a defended obstacle, to include the reduction of a pillbox; practice co-ordination with adjacent sections; become accustomed to advancing under fire of supporting weapons; and to co-ordinate movement with such fire*".

Medical staff, anti-tank platoons, engineers, infantry, tanks and anti-aircraft units all had their own mission with great emphasis upon amphibious operations. Communications troops were promised new radio sets for the invasion so considerable time was devoted within the training schedule for operators to become familiar with them. Infantry companies had two radio operators, one shadowed the company commander toting an SCR 300 back pack weighing about 20 pounds. This was efficient up to a mile and a half but any topographical interruption rendered it almost useless. The SCR 536 walkie-talkie radio was judged next to useless in almost any situation.

While deliberations to produce this firm doctrine had been taking place, negotiations to secure a suitable training ground had also been under way, but it hadn't been easy. All good training areas had already been claimed by the British so Thompson had no choice but to accept the Atlantic coast around Woolacombe, a coastline the British judged too rough and stormy for training. Thompson despatched Major Allen G. Pixton with three colleagues to view the discarded British site to assess its suitability for American uses. Pixton remembers that journey "*we travelled in a British Army sedan with a female soldier driver. At that time there were no road or direction signs in all of England so we had a difficult time finding our way to Woolacombe*". But as their site investigation concluded, it became clear that Woolacombe was absolutely ideal for the ATC's intended purposes. Beach characteristics and size, rise and fall of the tides, harbouring for naval craft, suitable inland terrain, and it was conveniently accessible for the American divisions to be trained as most were already quartered in the south west peninsula.

The boundary of the land Thompson required for full-scale military manoeuvres followed the railway line south from Mortehoe Station to Braunton, then tracked the River Caen to the Taw and Torridge estuary. Every acre to the west of this line he needed for exercises and rehearsals using live ammunition, explosives, tanks, artillery and air support. But nestling in this region were several peaceful, picturesque Devon villages – Croyde, Putsborough, Georgeham and Saunton. The task before Thompson at this stage included not only the neutralisation of enemy beach defences, but also the fight inland off the beaches, and these settlements were in his way. To emphasise his dilemma he submitted his own sketch concluding they would have to be evacuated along with all the farms and smaller settlements. His reasoning was these villages … *"lay squarely astride, and largely block, the two most important of the three or four natural corridors of attack. We must have at least maneuver rights through these villages, and preferably they should be evacuated. We must have freedom of action in the corridors which these villages occupy"*.

Outright evacuation was deflected by the American High Command, telling him he just had to be careful with live firing. Major General H.C. Ingles, Deputy Commander of the American European Theatre of Operations had written …*"With reference to our conversation re the evacuation of towns in the Woolacombe-Georgeham proposed training area, it will not be necessary to evacuate these towns. Such firing as may be done in this area will be limited and carefully controlled. After this area is occupied and in general use, we may find that it is necessary to ask the British Government to evacuate some of the towns therein, but no steps need be taken in the matter at present"*.

Thompson was insistent that to successfully and completely carry out his mission, there was no other option but to evacuate these villages. After weeks of frustrating inactivity and negotiations with civil servants of the British Land Requisition Directorate, it seemed to Thompson that the British were dragging their heels, depriving him of

Tent city.

precious time to activate his training base and his urgent memoranda prompted no response whatsoever. He was being pressed to establish the Assault Training Centre, but without confirmation he could use the land he wanted, he could make no plans. Thompson resorted to unconventional methods to resolve the stalemate by asking an influential high ranking American officer with access to the British Prime Minister to put his case. It was, but a few curt words from the Prime Minister to his civil servants upon their tardy performance produced quite the opposite to the desired effect and Thompson had to plead for negotiations to be resumed. By now he had lost an estimated two to three weeks in the whole programme.

Unexpectedly he was advised that his mission had been reduced. He no longer had to teach troops to fight their way inland past the enemy beach defences, just get them through the coastal fortifications. There were several reasons for this dramatic change. The American High Command had found an alternative area where amphibious-landed troops would assume the beach defences had been overcome, and could practice establishment of a bridgehead and moving inland.

That area lay just behind Slapton beach in South Devon. A more sinister reason for curtailing Thompson's initial two-fold mission was the higher command's revised estimates of casualty rates which they now believed would leave the assaulting units fully spent after the assault, and establishment of the bridgehead would have to rely upon rapid reinforcement. The mission reduction however was a relief for the ATC staff who could now concentrate their efforts to organise and write training programmes, lessons, exercises and practical problems for the infantry and engineers in their individual and combined tasks to hit the enemy shore and break through the crust of beach defences.

Eventually the land was officially handed to the Americans but before any construction could take place American army engineers had to locate and clear British mines scattered along the shoreline during the 1940 fear of a German invasion. The overall reservation boundaries remained as originally drawn but now, after the mission reduction, contained areas not needed by the military, so only those that would see action had boundaries drawn around them and were letter-coded.

The existing road network of narrow country lanes was assessed for movement of troops, trucks and tanks, some being so narrow for military traffic they were designated one-way. For ease of navigation road junctions were numbered, and where no roads existed new temporary tracks were constructed. Nearly all temporary roads laid by the U.S. Army have now been removed, although there are several complete examples still remaining in isolated areas. Their method of construction was typically American – quick, simple and effective. After grading the route, bitumen sheeting was laid with steel mesh on top, secured laterally and along the edges with steel strips securely pegged along the entire length. They were of adequate width to take a six wheeled truck, and strong enough to carry all the heavy construction vehicles necessary to maintain the training aids.

Beaches within the reservation were ideal for basic and advanced amphibious exercises despite the fierce Atlantic surf, and Woolacombe Sands was soon found to be identical to "Omaha" in nearly every respect of sand quality, beach gradient, and tide range. Major Russ

Finn remembers "*when I first saw the beach (Woolacombe) I thought I was in California or Florida. It seemed to be an ideal vacation site*".

Training troops to successfully overcome enemy beach defences required ranges for all weapons that would be used in the assault to ensure proficiency in handling, accuracy and repeated exercises in tactics of the new doctrine against accurate replicas of what they would encounter on the enemy shore. Construction of these ranges and training aids – mostly replicas of German pillboxes – had to be done quickly as the training schedule already drawn up had the first units arriving in North Devon on 1st September 1943. To build them U.S. Army Southern Base Section had assigned the 398th Engineer General Service Regiment who had only just arrived in England ... *"On August 7th we located ourselves on a hill a mile west of Braunton, North Devon. In fields bounded by stone walls, we pitched our pup tents for the first time on European soil. At night we learned that English soil was no softer than that found in United States on bivouac problems. With issuance of construction missions, Companies were scattered in all directions. Companies C and E were located one and two miles, respectively, west of Braunton. Company D established itself one mile north of Bideford. Company F set up camp a half mile south of Croyde. And Second Battalion Headquarters operated from Saunton Sands".* The 398th were hard pressed to complete their work in North Devon as they were urgently required on other construction assignments elsewhere throughout Great Britain.

With winter looming, a permanent camp was needed and just outside Braunton the 398th constructed ... " *505 Nissen huts for quarters, dispensaries, showers, ablutions and mess halls to comprise a camp capable of housing 4250 men. We laid 5000 feet of sewer line and 8700 feet of water line".* But by mid-October the camp was still only 65% completed with an estimated completion date at the end of that month, ready for the 115th Regimental Combat Team troops to take up residence. By early November the British weather was so bad that the roads were becoming rough, deteriorating and mud was becoming the number one problem. Braunton Camp was ... "*a sea of mud and utilities are far from complete. Only two companies of engineers are working on it. Colonel Thompson ordered two companies of the 234th*

Engineers to assist the 398th. He also found where a greater supply of rock was available and arranged to ferry truckloads thereof on LCTs". Five days later it was reported "*Braunton Hut Camp is still decidedly deficient in all mechanical equipment and services. The sewage system is doubtful and the roads are definitely inadequate. Colonel Thompson felt alternative camp facilities had better be available for the next RCT and made provisions to move tents to dry sandy areas*". These camps were for enlisted men at Lincombe above Woolacombe, Croyde behind the beach, and in fields inland from Braunton Burrows. The ATC staff consisting of 55 officers and 45 enlisted men moved from London to Woolacombe on 17th August 1943 and enjoyed more permanent accommodation. Major Pixton remembers "*there were five of us Majors who roomed with a Mrs. May in her home (Woolacombe). She was a delightful Scottish lady and was very nice to us during the time we were living in her home from July 1943 until the Spring of 1944*".

The Assault Training Centre had a progressive, fluid policy based on the early receipt of intelligence on German beach defences so they could immediately produce counter tactics. As a consequence of this constant up-dating, layouts of some training aids were altered, some added to, others removed or even abandoned between September 1943 and March 1944. The 398th Engineers had moved on before units arrived for training and their place was taken by the 146th Engineer Combat Battalion assuming the responsibility of maintenance and construction of the entire site. They found it took too long to replace or repair replica pillboxes that were constantly being attacked, damaged or destroyed by troops under training so devised an alternative. Concrete "faces" – pillbox sized solid concrete blocks with a sculpted or painted embrasure as an aiming point. These could be quickly and easily repaired by the simple application of an additional layer of concrete to the damaged area.

CHAPTER THREE
WEAPONS & OBSTACLES

THE Assault Training Centre's London conference had formulated not only the doctrine to be used against the enemy held coastline, but in doing so specified the number and type of weapons that were to be used by troops in that new amphibious assault doctrine. U.S. forces used two bolt action rifles but their standard weapon was a self-loading rifle – the M1 Garand. It performed well under rough conditions, and one practical advantage of this rugged design was that the gas operated reloading mechanism could be stripped and re-assembled using only the point of a bullet. Fed from an eight round magazine it could fire at the rate of thirty rounds a minute.

The Browning Automatic rifle, or BAR, dated from the First World War and was a semi-automatic weapon fitted with a bipod that was cumbersome in weight and length and a limited magazine of twenty rounds. At the Assault Training Centre it was often substituted for a light machine gun and was *"nearly always the case"* according to Major Robert M. Miller, "K" Company commander of the 29th Infantry Division.

Two types of hand grenade were used. The "A1" fragmentation grenade with grooves in the cast iron body to allow fragmentation and gave a better grip when throwing it and the M15 smoke grenade filled with white phosphorous, which created a localised smoke screen as intended but also became a useful anti-personnel weapon.

The "Bazooka" M9 A1 type had an electrical magneto firing mechanism in the pistol grip and made of aluminium to save weight it

Pole charge.

had a calibre of 3 inches and fired a hollow charge warhead which could penetrate most side and rear armour at a limited range. Principally an anti-armour weapon, the Assault Training Centre recognised the potential of firing a projectile through the embrasure of a pillbox to quickly neutralise it or cause the occupants to close the embrasure. Either result aided the Assault Section to approach the structure and demolish it.

Flamethrowers developed rapidly during the war, from a 70 pound, three cylinder back pack in 1942, to the M1A1 version of two fuel tanks and a smaller gas tank feeding the ignition. By early 1944 the M2-2 version came into service. It was lighter and more reliable but with a reduced range of just over 30 yards and a life of about 10 seconds.

Mortars were used in many calibres but for the Assault Section the 60 mm was ideal, weighing 43 pounds and firing a 2.9 pound bomb to almost 2,000 yards. Heavier calibres were expected to fire smoke from landing craft to create a screen for the Assault Sections.

Bangalore torpedoes were used to blow gaps in barbed wire or blow a path through a minefield. A simple British invention, they were metal tubes filled with explosive and could be linked together. By D-Day

Bangalore torpedo.

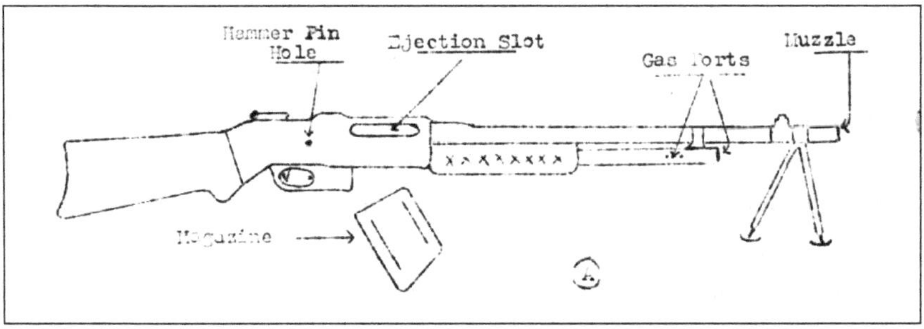

Browning Automatic Rifle.

there were considered obsolete by the British who had developed more sophisticated means of blowing gaps in wire entanglements but they were ideal for the ATC tactics.

These were the weapons distributed among sub-teams of an Assault Section, all required to engage, approach and assault an enemy pillbox to neutralise it. Not to destroy it but to subdue it, force it to cease firing under the attack and close the doors and embrasures to enable the demolition sub-team to rush forward and place demolition charges in vulnerable spots to destroy it.

Demolition teams used "Pole Charges", simply ½ pound TNT blocks taped to a ten inch square board on a swivel headed pole. The intention being that a demolition team member would run forward

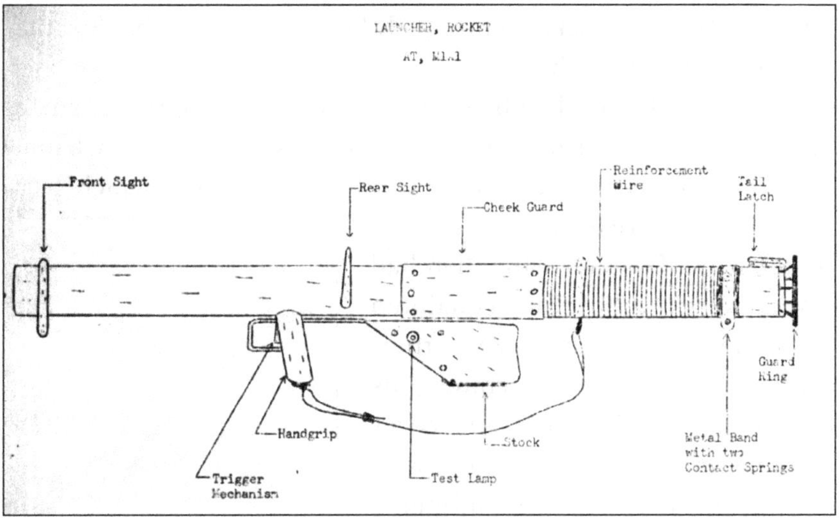

Bazooka.

U.S. ASSAULT TRAINING CENTER, ETOUSA ~~R-E-S-T-R-I-C-T-E-D~~

PROPOSED ASSAULT SECTION RIFLE CO (ASSAULT) BN LNGD TEAM (ASLT)	Personnel	Pistol	Rifle M-1	Carbine	Grenades Clrd Smoke	Grenades Smoke	Grenades Fragment	Launcher, Grnde	Bangalore	Wire Cutters	MG, cal .30, light	Amm, MG, boxes	Mortar, 60mm	Amm, 60mm, rds	Launcher, rocket	Rocket, AT	Pole Charge	Pack Charge	Grapnel	Flame Thrower	Signal Equip	Weight per man
Officer	1	1			4		2															12
Assistant Leader	1		1				8															27
Support Team **Riflemen** **Wire Cutters**	9 (5) (4)		5 4			14 4	12	1	2 8	2 4									3 2			29 33 53
LMG Team **Gunner** **Bearers**	4 (1) (3)	1		3							1	6										46 50
60mm Mortar Team **Gunner** **Bearers**	4 (1) (3)	1		3									1	36								46 45
Rocket Team **Rocketeer** **Assistants**	4 (2) (2)	2		2											2	16 20						47 42
Flame Thrower **Demolition Team**	2 5	1	1	 5		4 5	6 10										 5	 5		1		72 29 40
TOTALS	30	6	11	13	4	27	38	1	10	6	1	6	1	36	2	36	5	5	5	1		

Ammunition: 96 rds per M1 Rifle = 1056
60 rds per Carbine = 780
21 rds per Pistol = 126

U. S. Assault Training Center
18 Sept 1943

Weapons, ammunition and explosives.

once a pillbox had "buttoned up", lodge it against a door or embrasure, ignite the time fuse and rapidly retire.

These were the weapons and tactics to be used by the infantry against enemy defence constructions such as pillboxes, bunkers and reinforced emplacements immediately behind the beach, but first they had to get off the beaches.

As soon as France had been overrun in May 1940 the Germans had carried out detailed topographical surveys of the French Channel coastline, identifying all the natural strong points which were reinforced to create a deadly chain of defences. The Germans then had several years to become acquainted with the area, time to zero their artillery, mortars and machine guns across the open beaches and cover weak spots with minefields and wire entanglements. Every draw and gulley, every valley and stream bed leading inland off the shore was covered by fire from concrete pillboxes. In one four mile stretch of "Omaha" beach alone there were 128 defensive positions. In front of them on the sand were mile upon mile of parallel lines of anti-invasion obstacles of steel and concrete. They were monstrous steel and concrete traps designed to ensnare and repel any seaborne assault and slow their advance allowing defenders to destroy them by concentrated overlapping arcs of fire. The task of blowing gaps in these obstacles to allow landing craft to reach the shore lay with the combat engineers.

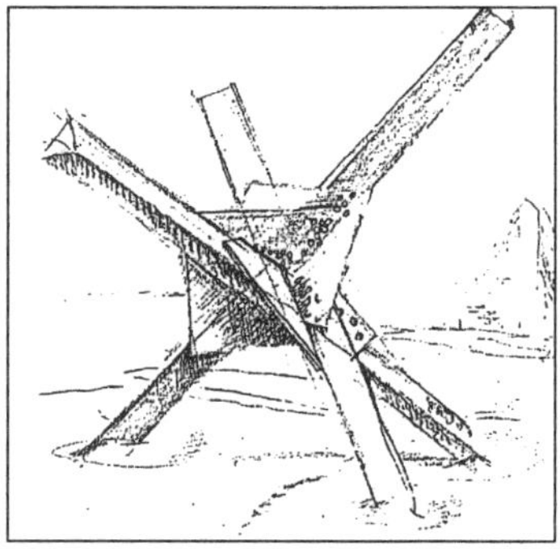

Hedgehog.

Czech Hedgehogs were one of the most common of German beach defences, intended to disembowel and sink landing craft and as an anti-tank obstacle. Constructed of three 4 foot lengths of heavy gauge steel angle, two secured in a cross with a bracing plate and the third at right angles through this centre plate and sometimes topped with a "Teller" anti-tank mine.

Tetrahydra were constructed of heavy gauge angle iron or concrete, standing about 4 ½ feet high with a triangular base forming a three sided pyramid topped with a spiked steel cap to disembowel landing craft and as an anti-tank obstacle.

Mined stakes were one of the simplest anti-invasion obstacles, seven feet long, angled seawards just under the high tide level. Some were topped with a "Teller" anti-tank mine secured by quarter inch

Ramps.

steel bands and fitted with a strong spring to prevent the sea from detonating the mine. Others had a serrated steel blade to cut open landing craft.

Timber ramps were twenty foot long heavy timbers inclined seawards supported by a ten foot high upright and a shell attached to the peak with the intention of impaling landing craft.

Element "C" also known as "Belgian gates" were constructed of six inch steel girders in a form ten feet wide, fourteen feet deep with cross braces and three ten foot high horns to tear open landing craft.

Fortifications and defences fronted by obstacles presented a seemingly impregnable line and the attacking Americans had to fight their way past and through these obstacles before confronting pillboxes and bunkers. The doctrine conference had realised the importance of tanks in the initial assault to support the infantry although their presence in the very first waves wasn't calculated into the Infantry Assault Sections' method of dealing with enemy pillboxes. Tanks would be in separate craft from the infantry and scheduled into initial support waves. Several methods of communication between tanks and infantry was tried as radio channels wouldn't mesh so tanks were instructed to support their nearest Assault Section when they would have a target designated by red coloured smoke and signed off that target by a green coloured grenade.

CHAPTER FOUR
ASSAULT SECTION

THIS was the very backbone of the Assault Training Centre's whole doctrine. It comprised of thirty infantrymen, divided into eight teams, each trained in specific skills and together, practised to work as a self-contained unit. The Assault Section was ... "*designed for frontal attack upon enemy fortified position, depending upon a system of coordinated fires to advance a highly specialized group to destroy the enemy fortifications. Enemy fires from other sources are neutralized by means within the section (mortar). The section is not designed for thorough mopping up but for breaching the enemy "crust" of defense*".

Amphibious operations were new to nearly every soldier attending the Centre, so alongside the usual safety regulations for waterborne

Assault Section.

Bazooka team.

Demolitiom team.

Machine gun.

Mortar team.

operations, it was considered essential to give instruction on how to wear combat equipment while aboard landing craft, in the event they should find themselves in deep water and need to discard their equipment. So concerned were the ATC in this respect that Colonel Brewster recalls "*The Center devised a special assault jacket. It could be easily jettisoned, if necessary. It was designed to hold a large amount of equipment, such as grenades and explosives. A model was flown to the States for manufacture. The British lacked facilities. 12,000 were manufactured, and sent to England, in less than 20 days. They were used on beach assaults. They were delivered about 10 days before D-Day*".

Wirecutting team.

Training Memorandum ASLT – 18 listed what each soldier should carry, including :-

ORGANIZATION : Each Assault Section is commanded by a lieutenant, who is the section leader; he is assisted by a sergeant, second in command of the section. The section itself consists of the following sub-teams; riflemen, wire-cutters, rocketeers, flame throwers, mortarmen, machine gunners, and demolition men

SUBTEAMS OF THE ASSAULT SECTION IN ACTION : The subteams of the assault section are organized and equipped to advance the demolition party to the vicinity of the pillbox, where it puts the pill-box out of action by placing explosive charges in vulnerable portions of the pill-box. The assault team is loaded into an LCVP (landing craft, vehicle and personnel) in a prescribed order which will permit the members of the team to debark in the following prescribed sequence:

The Section Leader – Riflemen – Light machine gun team – Mortar team – Wire cutting team – Rocket team – Flame thrower team – Demolitions team

DEVELOPMENT UPON DEBARKATION : Immediately upon debarking covered by smoke from the chemical mortars firing from landing craft, the section leader and riflemen move straight to the front in a rough V formation with about ten yards interval and about five yard distance between riflemen. The light machine gun team and the mortar team deploy to the left in that order with similar intervals and distances, in accordance with the procedure set forth in individual assault pamphlets. The wire cutting team, the flame throwing team and demolitions team initially deploy to the right in a similar fashion while the two launcher subteams deploy within the "V" about twenty yards apart and about twenty yards behind the section leader.

STEPS IN THE ASSAULT :
a. The section leader. Prior to the beaching of the landing craft, naval and aerial bombardment, have cratered the beach and full advantage of these shell and bomb craters is taken in the initial movements of the assault section. The assault section leader looks for the principal enemy fortification in his zone of action and for supporting enemy emplacements. He establishes communication with his supporting tank or gun by visual signal. He locates the elements of his assault section. Covered by the fire of the riflemen he moves forward locating possible points for breaching enemy obstacles, blind areas in the enemy fields of fire, etc. He causes routes to be marked out to these designated places by the riflemen, and he controls his section by prearranged signals, time schedules, phase signals, visual signals (usually arm and hand) and oral orders. The last two methods because of noise, smoke and difficulty of movement will be rarely successfully employed; emphasis must be laid on coordination of movement.

b. The assistant Leader. The assistant leader, a non-commissioned officer is the last man off the landing craft. He assists the section leader; is prepared to take the section leader's place, if the latter becomes a casualty; keep informed of the general situation at all times; and is particularly charged with the responsibility of locating covering fires from open emplacements and bringing mortar fire to bear upon such enemy installations.

c. The Light Machine Gun Team. The light machine gun squad takes position well to the flank of the assault section, where it can fire upon enemy installations taking care not to mask the fire of the supporting tank or gun. Should its fire be marked by advancing riflemen, the gun is moved to a new position from which the original target can be engaged. Short bursts of two or three rounds will be fired at the embrasure; however, the chief use of the machine gun will be in neutralizing fire from enemy open installations.

d. The Mortar Team. The mortar team moves to a position where it can bring fire on possible targets with maximum protection; they will receive orders from the assistant section leader to bring fire on open emplacements, but may direct fire on such emplacements at his own initiative. Fire is directed until the successful conclusion of the assault, when the mortar is prepared to fire on enemy concentrations and to break up enemy counterattacks.

e. The Rocket Launcher Team. The rocket launcher team moves up under the protecting fires of the riflemen, the machine gun and the accompanying tank until it reaches a position from which it can fire upon the embrasure. Rocketeers should take positions so that they are no nearer one another than twenty yards and where if possible communication can be established with the section leader. Fire is opened on the pillbox with armor piercing rockets to cover the advance of flamethrower and the demolitions party. When the flamethrower signals "I am ready", by arm and hand signal, the rocket fire is lifted. At the successful assault, the rocketeers advance to the next position or to attack a new pillbox as directed.

f. The Flame Thrower Team. The flame thrower team moves forward by short bounds, taking full advantage of cover, under the covering fires of the riflemen, the machine gun, the accompanying tank, and the rocket party until it reaches a point from which it can bring fire to bear upon the embrasure of the enemy pill-box. The assistant flame thrower keeps close contact with the demolition party, and when that party is in position to begin its assault, he signals to the rocketeer, "I am ready", by arm and hand or other pre-arranged signal, whereupon the rocket fire is lifted. The flame thrower party then opens with jets of one or two seconds and covers the placing of charges in the vulnerable points of the embrasure by the demolitions party.

g. The Demolitions party. Is "ball carrier" of the assault section for whom all the other teams do the "blocking". It works its way forward under the protective fires of the other weapons until it is ready to make the final movement to place the charges to destroy the pill-box. At this time, the leader of the party signals to the flame thrower party, "I am ready". The flame thrower then opens fire, and under the protecting jet, the demolition party places the necessary charge or charges in the vulnerable portions of the embrasure.

Men of the "Infantry Assault Teams" had to be at the peak of physical fitness, and to monitor this they were subjected to strength and endurance tests known as "burp-up" exercises. Passing this earned them the "Expert Infantryman's Badge" and an extra $10.00 in their monthly pay, failure resulted in a transfer to a non-combat unit. To qualify for this coveted badge the 100 yard run had to be made in12 seconds, doing 35 push ups and 10 chin ups, completing the obstacle course within the target time as well as qualifying on pistol, rifle and machine gun ranges. Some found this relatively easy to achieve and a limited amount of cheating was ignored to retain suitable men.

All training was deliberately carried out using live ammunition and explosives as noted by 1st Lt Gordon S. Ierardi during his fact finding visit ... "*The training undertaken at the Assault Training Center is undertaken most seriously and at times is definitely hazardous. Training with live ammunition presents a real problem. The problems (training exercises) must be intense enough to acquaint the participating troops with actual battle conditions and indicate to them proper methods of self-defense but on the other hand, they must not be so intense as to frighten the individual soldier and injure his fighting spirit. The Center Makes every effort to achive this goal and I believe that they achieve their aim. However occasional violent accidents are unavoidable*".

AREA "A"

BRAUNTON Burrows, a vast expanse of shifting sand dunes and slacks contained all the live-firing ranges and dummy pillbox clusters where infantrymen were taught step-by-step, the individual tasks of their sub-team and once mastered they progressed onto exercises and practical problems alongside the other sub-teams as a fully co-ordinated "Assault Section".

Area "A" as the most southern part of Braunton Burrows was the earliest area used with many ranges being abandoned in favour of larger or more sophisticated versions further north. Containing

Assembly area.

many structures associated with elementary lessons of vessel embarkation, loading and debarkation highlights the Assault Training Centre's emphasis on swiftly familiarising infantry soldiers with the amphibious element of a beach assault and these lessons were first on the training schedule of every unit. The location of the embarkation beaches dictated the position of the practice areas to be behind Broadsands on open, undulating sand dunes measuring 450 yards by 200 yards containing scale outlines of LCVPs and LCMs marked with poles where troops and vehicles practised embarking and debarking. According to the 1943 lesson plan, this mock up area ... "*simulates the boat waves afloat and its use familiarizes the troops with the positions of the craft in the (assault) formation. Its primary use is for training sections to take individual positions in craft and deploy therefrom*". Troops then moved to the assembly area for embarkation into the Navy's landing craft and their first experience of a short sea voyage.

Crow Point at the extreme southern tip is a half mile spit of sand jutting south eastwards into the sheltered waters of the Taw and Torridge estuary providing embarkation points onto landing craft for troops, tanks and vehicles. Crow Point and Broadsands to the east were divided into coded beaches. "Estuary Blue I and II", "Estuary Red II", "Estuary Green II" and "Estuary Yellow II", all provided a sheltered loading area whatever the weather or state of the tide and it was from these beaches that all landing craft embarkations took place, setting out seawards across the treacherous Bideford Bar, if it was negotiable, before heading north for landings on Saunton, Croyde or Woolacombe beaches.

Estuary Blue II beach extends along the north shore of Broadsands from the White House - where an American made slipway still exists - almost to the beach access road from Broadsands car park. At the top of the beach are remains of a lateral concrete wall and individual concrete beach obstacles, all showing evidence of explosion damage. Estuary Blue I beach runs along the seaward side of Crow Neck to Crow Point and has been totally eroded. Estuary Yellow II beach continues anti-clockwise from its boundary with Estuary Blue II beach, around the inside of Crow Neck to Crow Point and was covered to the low water mark with replicas of beach obstacles that would be

Broadsands.

Broadsands beach obstacles.

found in Normandy where trials were carried out to discover the most efficient method of destroying them.

Estuary Green II beach was on the eastern side of Crow Point where ... *"all embarkation of vehicles on either LCMs or LCTs will take place, using the North portion of Estuary Red II Beach to the extent necessary. No vehicles are permitted on the beach except to be embarked"*.

Cargo net.

On Friday 29th October 1943, First Lieutenant Gordon S. Ierardi - on a fact finding mission for the Adjutant General's Department - went to Crow Point and ... *"witnessed the embarkation of troops and tanks in LCVPs and LCTs which were going to take part in an assault exercise on Woolacombe Beach that afternoon. These craft are manned by the Navy who have a base at Appledore. As is usually the case, many of the landing craft were stuck on the beach after taking on their cargo of men or vehicles and had to be pushed into the water by the Army DUKWs. A very interesting case of the Army having to put the Navy afloat!"*.

Estuary Red II beach on the south eastern face of Crow Point was an alternative embarkation point to Estuary Green II beach, and also a practice area for embarkation, when ... *"during instruction periods on the beaches, or barge, vehicles will be parked in the parking area denoted "Vehicles to Embark Only" and embarkation will take place on Estuary Red II Beach"*.

Within the assembly area the Beach Embarkation Officer had an office in a nissen hut with a telephone line and microphone controlling the public address systems in the assembly and beach areas. The Beach

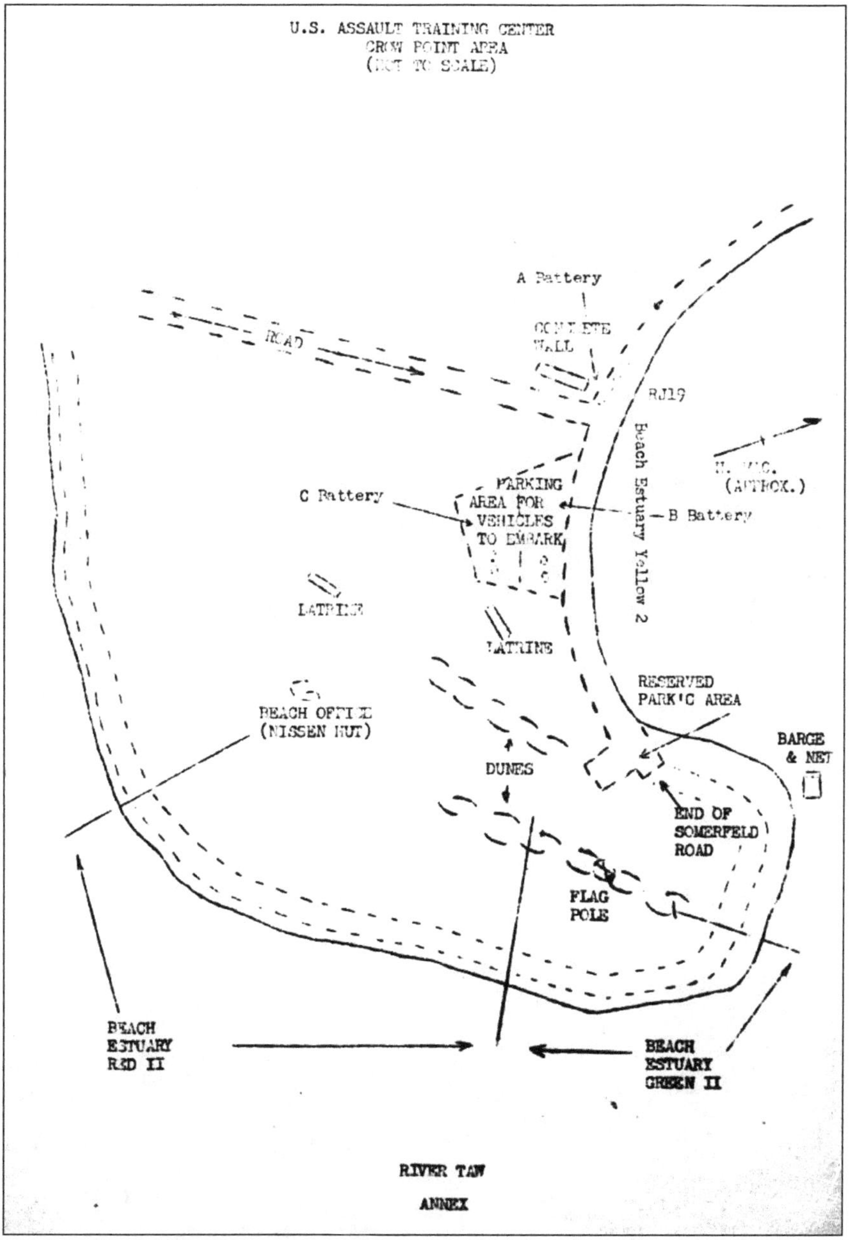

Crow Point.

Embarkation Officer would be notified by the Instructor or CO of the unit to be lifted, when ... "*the unit is ready for embarkation. Personnel to be embarked should proceed to the Assembly Area designated by the*

LCT mockup.

LCT mockup

dotted lines, where they will find boat section numbers, black on white background, set on posts. The numbers are arranged so that the sections can move across the dune line after call for embarkation with no, or very little, lateral movement by the best routes of march. Occupation of the assembly area and movement to craft on beach should be in orderly fashion. Light discipline is in force if embarkation is during darkness. The unit to be lifted will designate a Unit Embarkation Officer who will work in close co-ordination with the Beach Embarkation Officer at the Beach Office. On call from the Beach Embarkation Officer the boat team guides will report and procure their boat team signs. The Beach Embarkation Officer will call for the boat teams loading when he has been notified to do so by the Naval Beach master. Boat Team numbers are carried aboard craft at embarkation and placed in upright position with number visible. On landing, boat team numbers are carried off the craft and left on the shore above the waterline".

To the north of the LCVP and LCM mock up area, six concrete LCT (Landing Craft, Tank) mock ups were constructed which are still standing in various states of dilapidation. Tanks, trucks and artillery would master embarking and debarking on these concrete bases that represent LCTs with lowered ramps - as if they had just beached. The original bases were built to the dimensions of the Mk IV LCT, but as landing plans developed it became clear that the Mk V version would be used. Consequently additional aprons were added to the rear of existing bases to represent the extended deck area of the updated craft. Inscribed in wet concrete of one such extension is the mark of its constructors ... "*146 ECB, Co C, 1st Platoon*". While only the bases, jaws and ramps of the LCTs are represented - evidence exists that six-foot high scaffold poles stood around the edges with canvas curtains or corrugated metal sheeting hung between them to create the effect of the craft sides.

Area A introduced troops to the most basic initial elements of an amphibious assault, from scrambling over the side of a transport ship into landing craft and a short sea voyage. The Assault Training Centre instruction guide AMPH W-2 & W-3 listed the equipment that was to be carried by the troops for this training, including . . . " *BARs, HMG, wire cutters, 81mm mortars, 60mm mortars, Flame Throwers, simulated pole charges, satchel charges and bangalores* ". The general plan was to spend forty minutes demonstrating how to properly wear their equipment and then assign groups to their individual mock-ups for an hour of practising embarkation and debarkation. After this they reassembled and moved to the beach at Estuary Red II to embark on LCVPs and LCMs for a sea voyage to Croyde beach. On arrival, they were to debark as practised, and advance inland ... "*assuming light resistance*"for about three hundred yards.

LCT mockup.

A large wooden barge was grounded at the very tip of Crow Point, and although nothing today exists of this vessel, there have been some alarming finds of dummy hand grenades. Here the lesson split the trainees into four groups, which rotated through a twenty-minute demonstration of how a 30-man section should descend using nets and lower their equipment and trying for themselves before the first wave embarked on landing craft for the sea voyage to Croyde beach.

Between Crow Point and the town of Appledore across the estuary was moored the USS "President Warfield". As a Chesapeake Bay steamer she had peacefully plied her trade of ferrying cars and passengers between small harbours along the Virginia shoreline until the summer of 1942. Barry Dwyer, an American naval historian recalls her history ... "*The U.S. War Shipping administration claimed her, and after modifications she sailed for England with seven other ex-*

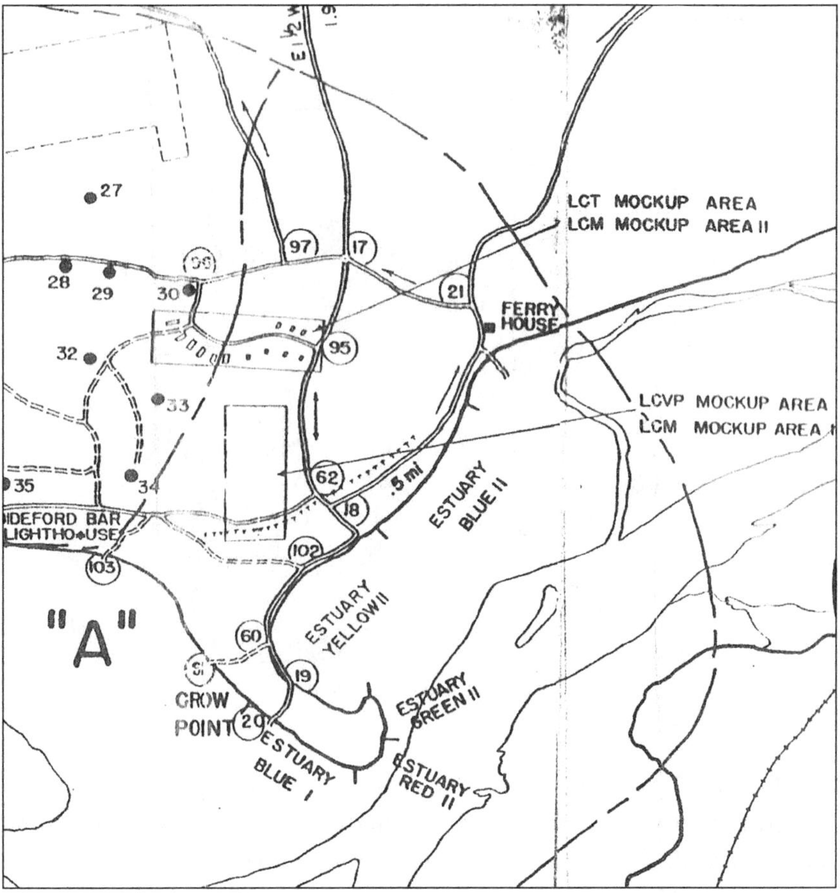

Map.

coastwise steamers per request of the British Ministry of War Transport. They sailed on 21st September 1942 and most fell victim to U-boat attacks, but the "Warfield" came through unscathed. For her first few months in England she was moored at Instow, Devon, where, fast in the mud at low tide she served as a Combined Operations training and barracks ship. In July 1943 the ship was reclaimed by the United States and became U.S.S. "President Warfield" (IX-169). In April 1944 she was moved to Barry Roads to continue her training role as an assault boat training base, crossing the Channel on D+30 to serve as a station and accommodation ship for harbour control. In 1947 "Warfield" began transporting Jewish emigrants to Palestine having been renamed "Exodus" by her new owners, and starred in the book by Leon Uris and the subsequent cinema film".

Troops in assembly area.

The U.S. Navy was vital to the Assault Training Centre's training programme but relations between them wasn't always harmonious as 2nd Lt William J Fox discovered when analysing the ATC notes … "*Colonel Thompson had noted in the past that there was difficulty in working things out with the Navy, but that now there seemed a greater understanding by the Navy of the Center's problems and less and less of an "it-can't-be-done" attitude. From the Center's standpoint, the Navy had appeared too hide-bound and wrapped in red tape, with a lot of its landing craft commanders – mainly young Ensigns – too cocky and immature for the authority vested in them*".

AREA "B"

OCCUPYING the south western part of Braunton Burrows, it contains some of the earliest constructions for assault training and a high proportion of unmarked and unidentified remains. One anomaly here is Churchill Plain – delineated as "out of bounds" to troops under training – it has yielded many finds including flame thrower tanks and mortar ammunition indicating it was in fact used for assault exercises.

Constructions known to be in the area include Ranges 19 to 35 inclusive and Range 52, all used by sub-teams of the Infantry Assault Section to learn and perfect their individual skills. Alongside training for the Assault Sections to neutralise enemy beach defences and establish a beachhead, engineers were trained for their task of clearing that beachhead of obstacles and minefields and to quickly create beach exits enabling reinforcements to take the assault inland. To achieve this, special ranges were dedicated to the engineers namely the Engineer Obstacle Course and Engineer Demolition Range specifically for obstacle demolition.

On the coastal boundary of Area "B" Beaches Estuary Yellow I, Estuary Green I and part of Estuary Red were colour coded for ease of identification but rarely used for beach landings although Airy Point, and road junction 94, were used extensively in medium scale landing exercises.

The Assault Training Centre's Diary Notes for 4th October 1943 records one such … *"Landing exercise held north of Airy Point. This is a hazardous area. One man was lost. The LCVPs are not doing well in the surf at the present stage of training of the crews. In this exercise there was decided congestion on the beaches. A naval beach party is needed and the junior officers should show more initiative in getting their units deployed and moved along. Colonel Thompson felt we were fortunate in not having more losses to date".*

The 116th Regimental Combat Team of the 29th Infantry Division undertook this ill-fated exercise having planned it themselves based upon information provided by the Assault Training Centre for Field Exercise Number 3, where it was to be assumed that … "*The western coast of DEVON is a section of the German held coast of NW FRANCE and the sector in which this exercise takes place is one of the more strongly defended sectors*".

Their summary of enemy information was intimidating … "*All pillboxes are surrounded by barbed wire, usually triple concertina with some double apron in evidence. This protective wire is generally about 50 yards from the pillbox or fortification. These pillboxes can usually be expected to be mutually supporting with interlocking bands of fire, which cover bands of tactical wire. They are also strongly defended by riflemen. The beach line has been heavily wired above the high water mark generally with two parallel bands of wire. Mines can be expected to be prevalent in the beach area above high tide, especially in the vicinity of the beach exits. The enemy is known to activate mines with booby traps and to make considerable use of trip wires. No evidence of underwater obstacles has been disclosed to date. The beach area can be expected to be heavily covered by both artillery and mortar fire. Latest estimates indicate that there are probably about two platoons of infantry manning the defenses in this sector. One Panzer division is located at EXETER, about 45 miles to the SE, and can close in the BARNSTAPLE BAY area by about H + 24*". For a touch of reality in this and many other exercises a defending force was … "physically *represented on the ground and will wear red hat bands".*

Reality and safety had both to be considered. Live demolition charges were used, but blank ammunition was issued with strict orders that … " *it will not be fired closer than 20 yds to personnel*". And … "*Physical contact between members of opposing forces is prohibited*". To ensure that all participants obtained the maximum training, casualties were not assessed but … "*In order to permit essential training of the*

Training range 28.

Airy Point.

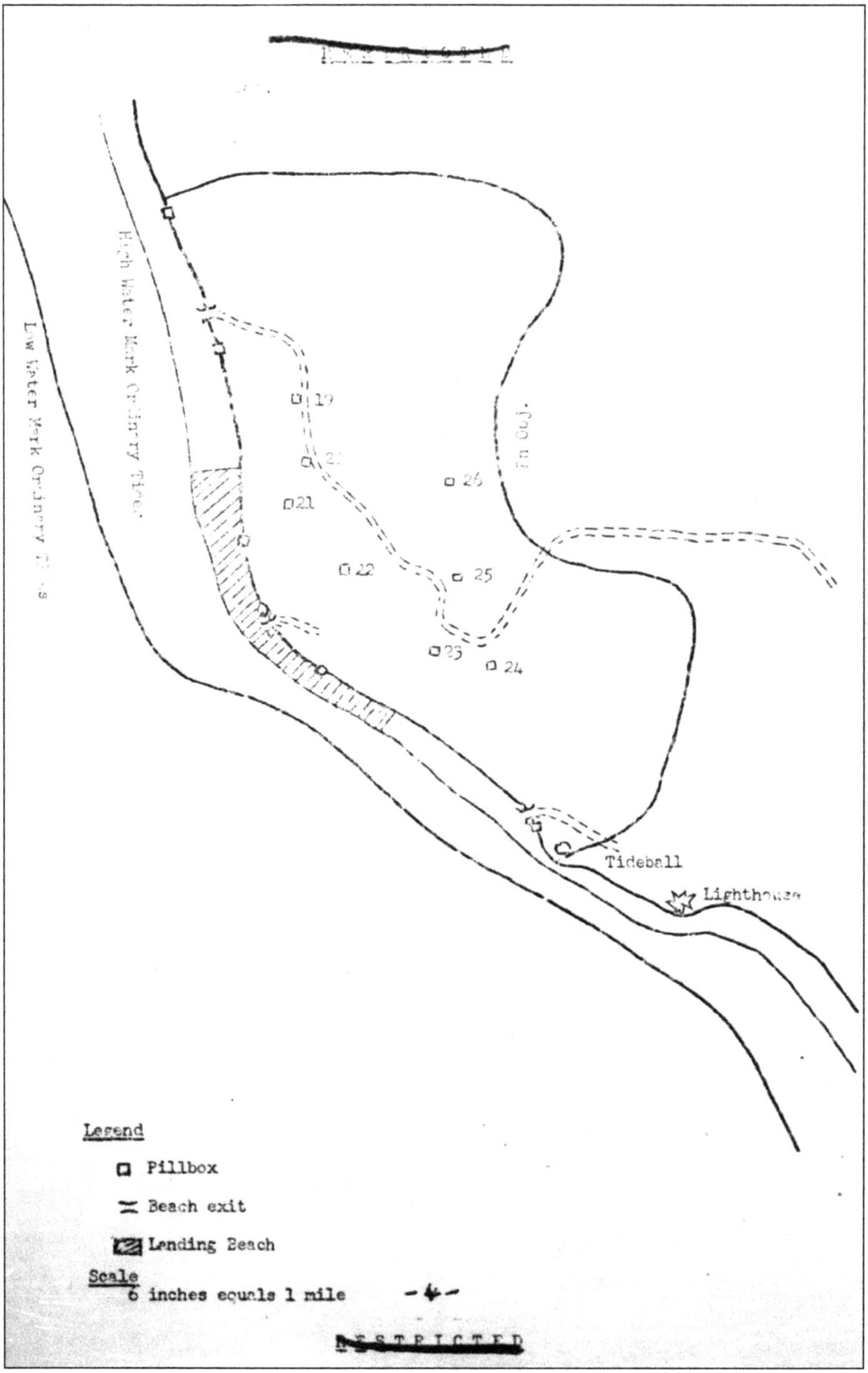
High Water Mark Ordinary Tides
19
21
22
25
26
23
24
Tideball
Legend
Pillbox
Beach exit
Landing Beach
Scale
6 inches equals 1 mile

Airy Point.

battalion medical detachment with the landing team, designated personnel of the defending forces at each pillbox will, after the pillbox has been assaulted, be tagged by the umpire at the pillbox, the tag showing the type of wound. The tagged personnel will remove their red hatbands and remain in vicinity of the pill-box, and thereafter emulate and be considered as casualties of the landing team and will be treated and handled by the medical personnel of the landing team as such".

Medical units were separately tested on their ability to treat and evacuate wounded men of a battalion landing team. Embarking in DUKWs at Crow Point beaches they travelled by sea to Airy Point with the exercise mission of landing, move inland along the battalion's axis of advance and treat wounded along the way, all against a tight time schedule. School troops were used as simulated casualties and were already tagged by a medical umpire and were to be treated by the advancing medical troops according to their tag. Litter cases were to be treated as such but, the exercise deliberately built in the case where no vehicles were available and casualties had to be hand stretchered back to the beach and loaded onto DUKWs.

It was known that barbed wire would be deployed as an outer defence to any fortification and it was essential to pass through this belt in order to attack the structure itself. Ranges 19, 20 and 21 were used to teach and practice breaching these wire entanglements. The

3. Concrete Obstacles

Obstacle	Description	Hand-placed charge	Placement	Minimum Safety Distance	Sketch
a. Reinforced Concrete Wall	10' high 8' thick	(1) Approximately 2 lbs C-2/ft^3 of gap desired.	Outline gap in U-shape w/3/4 of charge: place 1/4 in center.	100 yds	
b. R.C. cube, cylinder, or egg.	4' x 4' x 4'	2 packs C-2	On ground, on side.	50 yds	
c. R.C. coffin	3' x 3' x 5'	1 pack C-2	On ground midway of long side, against coffin.	50 yds	
d. R.C. Dragon's Teeth	6' high 3' high 2' high	(a) For individual teeth: 2 packs C-2 ½ pack C-2 ¼ pack C-2 (b) If base is above ground, see atchd Sketch "B"	On ground beside (a) tooth or (b) base	100 yds	

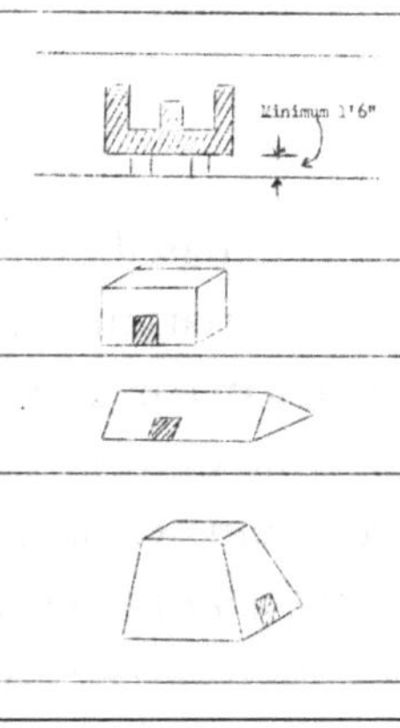

Chart 1.

4. Steel Obstacles

Obstacle	Description	Hand-placed charge	Placement	Minimum Safety Distance	Sketch
a. Rail obstacle (Timber post obstacle similar)	(1) R.R. sharpened, driven in upright or at 45° angle. (2) Bent Rail	1 block C-2 per footing	At foot of rail. Connect charges w/primacord. Charge in close contact with rail.	50 yds	
b. Steel Scaffolding.	2" Pipe barrier, with friction joints, made into frame 9' high.	Bangalore Torpedoes 10 lengths.	Tied to vertical and sloping main members.	100 yds	
c. Tetrahedrons	5 ft on a side; made of 6" steel members.	2 blocks C-2	Placed at all four corners. (1/2 block per corner)	50 yds	
d. HedgeHog	Three 6" x 6" steel members welded at center or with block of concrete cast at center.	1 block C-2	At center of cross. Close contact	50 yds	
e. Chevaux-de-Frise	Made of 2" steel tubing, covered with wire.	One length of bangalore.	Along main member.	30 yds (on axis of bangalore)	

(Continued on Page 4)

Chart 2.

4. Steel Obstacles (Continued)

Obstacle	Description	Hand-placed charge	Placement	Minimum Safety Distance	Sketch
f. Element "C"	Structural steel gate.	C-2 blocks at specified joints.	Place charges to cut all vertical members at top and bottom	50 yds	
g. Curved Rail	Structural steel rails.	Same	Same	50 yds	
5. Ditch Obstacles					
a. Triangular ditch.	Triangular cross-section	3 C-2 packs	Charges placed along ditch, on parapet.	25 yds	
b. Trapezoidal ditch		6 C-2 packs	Same, but placed on both sides of ditch	25 yds	
c. Ditch revetted with concrete, up to 1 ft thick.	Either cross-section	C-2 packs side by side across gap width.	On parapet or against revetted wall, 1/3 way up	50 yds	Charge or here
d. Covered ditch	Normal ditch with brick or wooden cover	Same. Use well-breaching data if concrete revetments over 1 ft thick.	Same, except for heavy concrete revetment.	100 yds	

Chart 3.

lesson plan dated 1st November 1943, coded A-7, was taught to the Rifle team within each Assault Section and covered bridging and tunnelling of barbed wire. The lesson was delivered to battalion sized groups who were first … *"given a demonstration by School Troops on use of tracing tape. Companies will then be assigned one per range with each No. 1 Rifleman assuming active control of his party. Entire group of 30 will work toward barrier using creeping or crawling method of advance. One party will, as designated, cut gap with cutters, bridge it, or tunnel it. When*

one party has completed this performance, groups will rotate". It was so important to get through the wire and close enough to attack the enemy pillbox that these lessons and practical problems were taught to all sub-teams even though there was a dedicated wire cutting team within each Assault Section.

One pillbox replica was at Range 28 but all that remains is a large mound with surface concrete debri and a long, deep ditch to one side that was probably a tank run along the southern edge of Churchill Plain.

Assault Training Centre Range 29 Grid reference: 45777-33317
Description: Concrete large debri

Assault Training Centre Range 30 Grid reference: 46080-33254
Description: Single steel bar

Assault Training Centre Range 31 Grid reference: 45538-32993
Description: Concrete remnants

Assault Training Centre Range 32 Grid reference: 45815-33045
Description: Concrete rubble

Assault Training Centre Range 33 Grid reference: 45972-32907
Description: Large concrete debri

Assault Training Centre Range 36 Grid reference: 45512-32827
Description: Surface rubble

Assault Training Centre Range 52 Grid reference: 45228-33398
Description: Concrete + wire

No trace has been found of Ranges 34 or 35

For engineers to achieve their mission they had to be convers with every type of obstacle they were likely to encounter and know how to destroy them. Their demolition range ran the length of Bo Slack – a perfect amphitheatre for explosions where the surrour high bluffs formed a natural safety barrier for the constant demc practice that went on here. Evidence suggests that lateral li different obstacle types stretched across Bomber Slack, comp

Dragons Teeth.

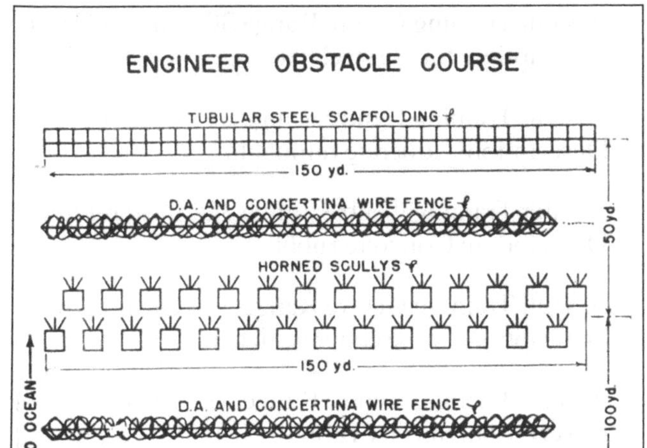

Engineer Obstacle Course.

Engineer Obstacle Course.

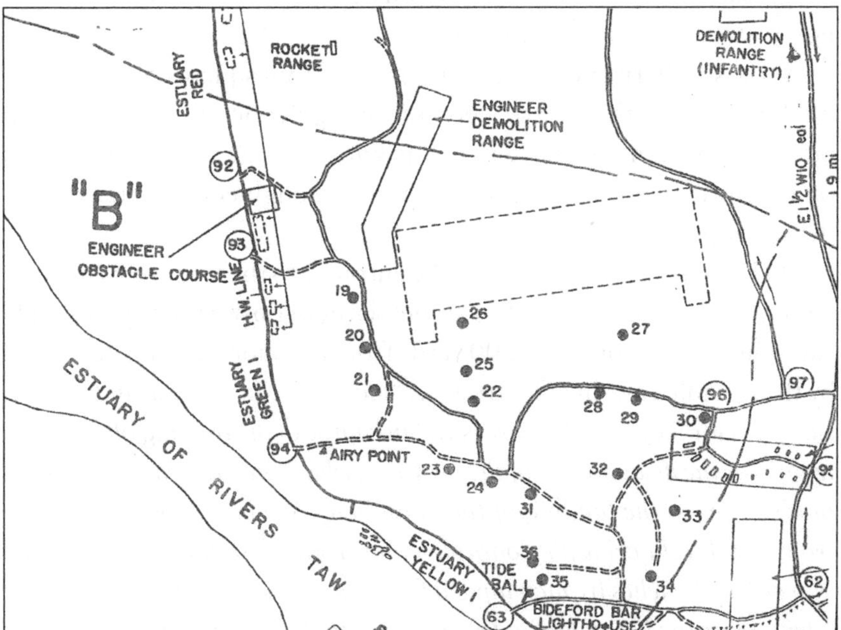

Map.

Beachmaster's hut base.

progressive forward movement from the site of the "Dragons Teeth" north eastwards along the slack.

At the southern end of this range lay a 50 foot square checker board of "Dragon's teeth". These were 4 foot high concrete pyramids – an effective anti-tank obstacle that was known to lay at many locations on the invasion beaches so it was vital that engineers practised their demolition.

On Estuary Green I beach lay the entrance to the Engineer Obstacle Course which comprised of a parallel series of obstacles 50 yards wide extending inland for about 200 yards from the shoreline and described by the Assault Training Centre as ... "*more difficult than any anticipated case*". Major Reginald Page was ... "*in charge of the training of Engineer troops for the assault wave of the invasion, whose mission was the removal of obstacles to the landing of the main body. We had good intelligence from low-level aerial photography, and from personal scouting of the Normandy beaches by men landed from submarines ... We got technical advice from the U.S. Chief of Engineers as to the quantity and placement of explosives*". To tackle this daunting course engineer troops would

Vista.

embark on landing craft at Crow Point for the short sea voyage to Estuary Green I beach where they would debark in the surf to assault the Obstacle Course. Working their way off the beach through the different belts of obstacles, their objective was to clear a path wide enough for a tank, for the entire depth of the course.

AREA "C"

SPANNING the whole central part of Braunton Burrows was in 1943 a flat, open sandscape compelling training ranges to be concentrated in the coastal strip of high dunes with all live firing to seaward.

Constructions known to be in Area C include Ranges 46 to 51, the Rocket Range, Infantry Demolition Range and beaches Saunton Blue, Saunton Yellow and part of Estuary Red.

Assault Sections spent a lot of their training time at these concrete faces and pillbox dummies using live ammunition in practice assaults each lasting an hour. More than one assault section took part at these sites so one could carry out its assault while the other took instruction on how to deal with anti-personnel mines and booby traps because training staff would place thundeflashes representing these in the line of attack.

A large concrete wall situated in Butts Slack was the target backdrop for "Bazooka" rockets fired from the floor of the slack beyond where contrasts in vegetation colour indicate foxholes and trenches used by the marksmen. Many Bazooka heads and fins have been found at the base of the wall, and nearby steel wreckage suggest whole vehicles were also used as targets in front of the wall. Training was spread over several lessons including characteristics of the rocket and launcher and three hours practice firing with dummy rockets from 50 yards and 75 yards in the prone, sitting and kneeling positions before progressing to live ammunition.

The Infantry Demolition Range is a large, flat and sometimes waterlogged area 100 yards wide, running south for some 300 yards

Face 47.

Face 49.

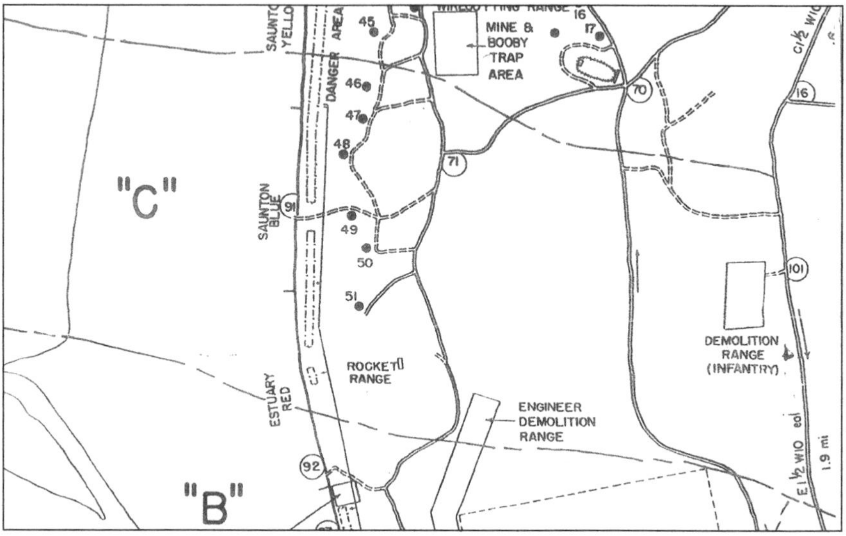

Map.

from Sandy Lane car park beside the American Road across Hog Wood Plain. Here demolition teams of five infantrymen learned and practised their new skills, starting from basic charge preparation through to constructing the specialised explosive packs they would use to subdue enemy fortifications and destroy beach obstacles. The entire assault doctrine revolved around this team's ability to successfully conclude the assault on an enemy fortification, and team members were especially selected from the ranks as being already proficient in their basic arms of carbine and hand grenade and judged to be level headed and reliable under fire. Teams under instruction would gather around the concrete obstacles they were to destroy, three walls all six feet high and of various thicknesses, to be shown how to prepare different types of explosives and primers. Each trainee had to satisfactorily prepare five explosive charges with primers and set them off against the concrete walls before progressing to the construction and use of satchel and pole charges.

It was known that to breach a 6-foot thick pillbox wall of reinforced concrete required around 400 pounds of explosive, so demolition parties hand placed their small charges in vulnerable points of a pillbox, the embrasures, door hinges and locks, and other weak spots such as angles in roof and walls and while it was recognised that these

Rocket wall.

Wall-Pole Charge.

would not destroy the pillbox, the concussion inside the fortification may temporarily neutralise the occupants long enough for a second, more damaging charge to be placed.

The Demolition Party had their own detailed instructions when landing … *"to advance as fast as possible behind the wire-cutting, Bazooka and flame thrower parties. When the objective is within range of the rocket launchers, all demolition men with the exception of one or two will remain under cover. The flamethrower party advances on signal, closely followed by one or two demolition men prepared to assist or even replace the flamethrower in case of necessity. The remainder of the party may follow in echelon. After the embrasure engaged has been forced to close up under the fire of the flame thrower, the first demolition man runs forward, in a blind spot, and places his first charge, pulls the fuse lighters, and dodges to the nearest cover. After a breach has been made, the occupants may be more fully liquidated by a satchel charge or hand grenade thrown into the breach".*

AREA "D"

THE northern part of Braunton Burrows contained the greatest concentration and diversity of assault ranges and training constructions being bounded on the landward side by small lanes, to the north by the road from Braunton to Croyde, and to the west by beaches, "Saunton Green, Yellow and Red".Within this area were ranges numbered 1 to 17 and 37 to 45, flamethrower and wire cutting ranges and the Hedgehog – site of the training course finale. Many of the lower numbered training ranges have not been located due to massive sand shifts and dense vegetation and little remains of the "Hedgehog" due to such comprehensive destruction during training. Many training aids were built on Saunton Golf Course including the Obstacle course and Ships Sides but have long been demolished or now lie buried beneath greens and fairways.

Facilities used by the Assault Training Centre were also available to units other than the seaborne invasion spearhead units under training and in April 1944 ... "*two groups of about 1000 men each from the 101st Airborne Division each received five days training. They were made up of composite units so that companies spread throughout the division would be trained. Again both the (ATC) staff and the 101st felt it was valuable and regretted that more of them were not able to be in on it. Their assault training did not include dropping or landing by glider and of course no amphibious work. It assumed they had reached the area of their objective and started from that point. They did not use the 30 man assault team (based on the capacity of the LCVP), but proposed teams of parachute infantry platoons consisting of two officers and 35 men and glider infantry platoons of one officer and 46 men. A special area was turned over to them*

Airborne troops' training area.

for their final assault problem and this was in the nature of a rehearsal. They showed exceptional energy and enthusiasm". That area is just east of Range 17 and was a replica of the German field artillery position at St Martin de Varreville in Normandy, one of the D-Day objectives of the 101st. Despite this detailed rehearsal, on D-Day airborne troops simply by-passed this position. Replicas of the German earthworks are shown in a 1946 aerial photograph appearing as "craters". There is nothing to be found here today except hardcore and rubble delineating the track that passed through the centre of what was a very boggy area. Just to the north was found a U.S. Army "dog tag" in the name of Howard A. Knight, service number 0-885740 but no trace can be found of this soldier.

Obstacle course.

Cargo net.

On Range 40 riflemen were lectured on the combat use of rifles before moving to range 39 to zero their weapons and demonstrate their marksmanship with 24 rounds on silhouette targets which was marked, scored and recorded. It was also used for mortar instruction, starting with lessons in identifying component parts of the weapon, ammunition functions, and sighting on open targets represented by large concrete cubes.

Ranges 41 and 42 were for sub-teams to practice their individual part in the reduction of enemy constructions but have been destroyed by post war military activity leaving only mounds of sand. The remains of Range 43 by contrast are a good example of a concrete "face".

Range 47 was the Machine gun range where gunners were taught the adaption of shell holes for machine gun emplacements and various methods of firing from cover.

Around the eastern edge of Saunton golf course were several training aids including the Obstacle Course and "Ship Sides". These were three huge scaffold towers, draped with cargo nets where troops Flamethrower.practiced their descent into landing craft.

Flamethrower.

The obstacle course was over 800 yards long, stretching over sand dunes in the shape of a horseshoe, travelling south taking a semicircular turn to the right before heading north so that the beginning and end of the course were only 100 yards apart. The course was ten yards wide and run in teams of five abreast. Originally it was designed to acquaint soldiers with obstacles that may be encountered on crossing the beaches but later additions included obstacles to be found onboard ship such as ships ladders and cargo nets. Not only was it a test of the troops' physical condition but it encouraged team work as well as individual proficiency and brought into play muscles neglected by the general physical training of an infantry division as arm, chest and stomach muscles were strengthened by tugging and pulling on walls, ladders and ropes.

OBSTACLE No. 1 & 8: Were concrete walls one foot thick, nine feet high and 30 feet long, comparable to tide or beach walls on French beaches. The five man team assisted each other in scaling them and descending the other side.

OBSTACLE No. 2: Barbed wire net 30 feet square and 18 inches above ground level, stretched over a 3 foot deep hole. Its purpose was to attempt to teach men to crawl through trenches and to move swiftly in a crouched position to afford as small a target as possible.

OBSTACLE No. 3: An overhead ladder with crossbars spaced 18 inches apart across the width of the course, 18 feet long and 8 feet above ground level, over a ditch, 4 feet deep, filled with barbed wire.

OBSTACLE No. 4: A ditch the width of the course, 9 feet across, 6 feet deep and filled with barbed wire was designed to give confidence to soldiers.

OBSTACLE No. 5: Set of three, 4 foot high hurdles simulating brick walls and fences that have to be crossed in street warfare.

OBSTACLES 6, 12 and 15: Three rolls of concertina wire stretched just 12 inches above the ground taught the proper method of crawling under wire to be cut and at the same time taught them to keep low on the skyline.

OBSTACLE No. 7: Logs 9 inches in diameter, 18 feet long over concertina wire was a balance test.

OBSTACLE No. 9 and 11: Confidence Jump, 9 feet down over barbed wire.

OBSTACLE No. 10: Cable Walk. Two parallel cables stretched across a 30 foot ditch, one cable 6 ½ feet directly above second cable was a balance, arm and confidence exercise.

OBSTACLE No. 13: Combination ship ladder and cargo net. Presented two devices that personnel would encounter on board transport ships, from hold to deck and cargo net over side.

OBSTACLE No.14: Swinging Bridge. A cable bridge with wood flooring was a balance test.

OBSTACLE No. 16: Rope Swing. An 8 foot rope hanging from a 12 foot high crossbar, over a 4 foot ditch was an arm and stomach exercise.

OBSTACLE No. 17: Bear Trap. Knee high wire entanglements kept soldiers foot conscious and wary of trip wires.

OBSTACLE No. 18: Sand bag wall. 5 foot high with ditch behind 4 feet wide and filled with barbed wire, a tiresome jump after ½ mile of running.

OBSTACLE No. 19: Balance Walk, a zigzag walk through barbed wire was a balance test after the ½ mile trip.

On the southern edge of Saunton golf course was the Flamethrower range. Four lessons and practical exercises were given, covering fuelling, waterproofing and cleaning the apparatus, and the correct approach to a pillbox.

Centrally placed in Area D was the "Hedgehog". The culmination of every three week training course resulted in this area being assaulted by the trainees tackling twelve individual obstacles or fortifications which had to be overcome by the Infantry Assault Teams assisted by tanks, artillery and air attack. 1st Lt Gordon S Ierardi's fact finding

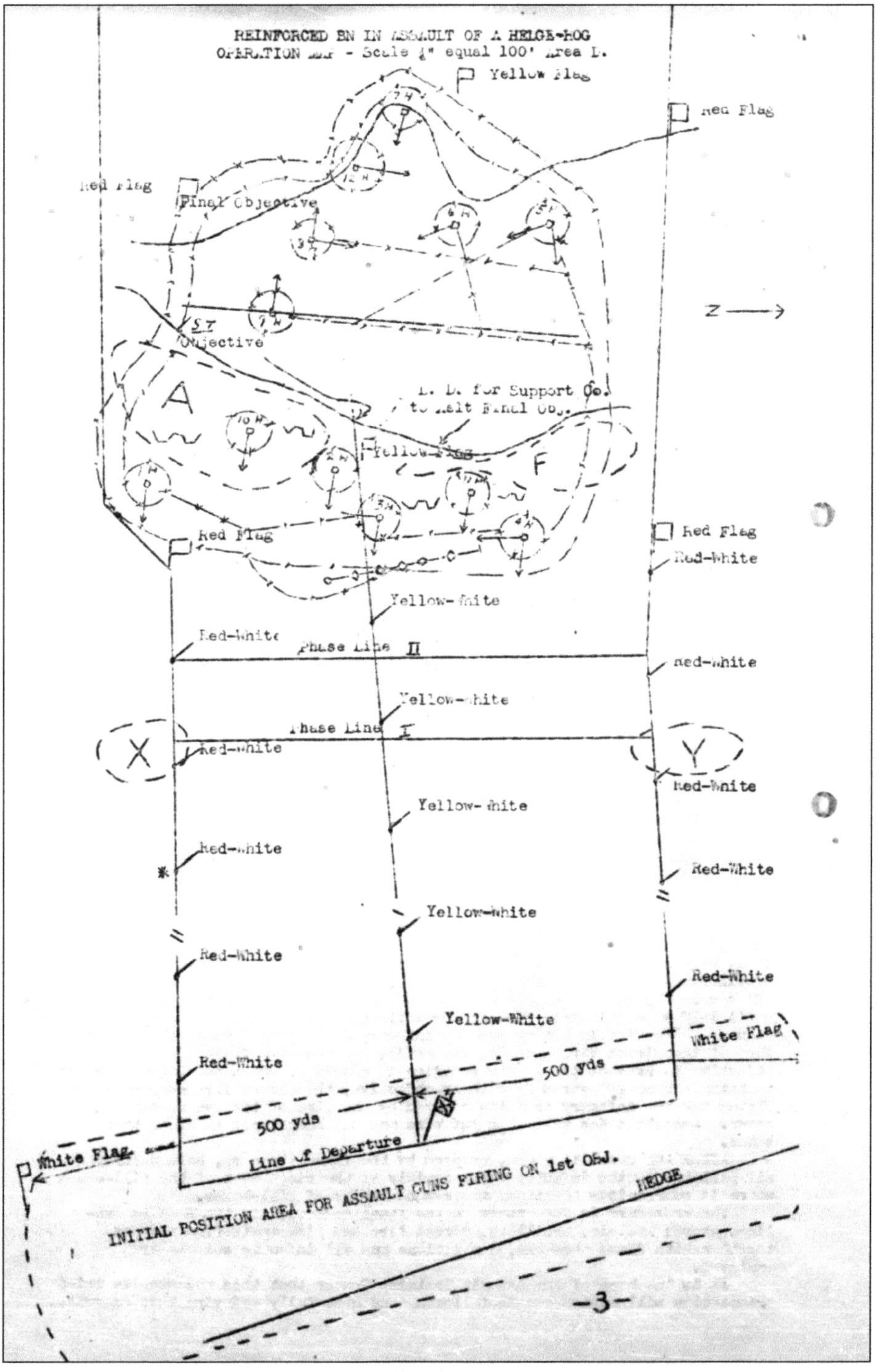

Hedgehog plan.

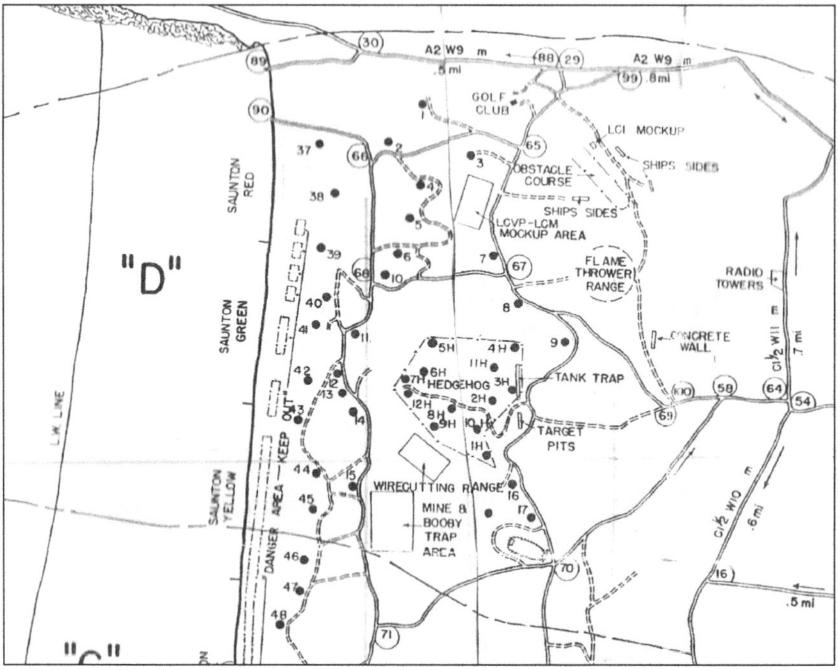

Map

Mortar range.

mission in October 1943 included watching a hedgehog assault ..."*This involved the use of foot troops and tank destroyers who assault and overwhelm two succeeding groups of pillboxes and hills. The exercise began at 1:30 with 105mm artillery laying down a barrage on the positions to be attacked. Three Spitfires then attacked the pillboxes, spraying them with a concentrated fire from their machine guns. The artillery then laid down a barrage of white phosphorous smoke shells which covered the scene. The 81mm and 60mm mortar crews then went into action, while the first wave of foot soldiers swept forward. They were well camouflaged with faces painted and foliage inserted in their helmet nets. As they crept ahead, the artillery of the tanks and tank destroyers went into action with their 3 inch guns. As the infantry moved closer to their objective they threw smoke grenades which concealed their further progress. As the arrived at the pillboxes, the assault platoons went into action, the wire cutting team, the Bangalore demolition team, the flamethrowers and the machine guns*".

On the wire cutting range instruction was not only given in the use of Bangalore torpedoes to blow gaps in barbed wire entanglements but included safe movement across minefields on the approach as it was known that German wire defences were preceded by anti-personnel minefields.

In December 1943 an analysis of ATC notes and diary entries were made by 2nd Lt William J Fox and found the course involving mines had been modified ... "*because it was felt our troops were becoming too mine-conscious, and as a result, over-cautious. It is felt that they must be more aggressive, take the risk with the mines not exploded on the beaches, and move forward quickly, avoiding the greater risk of remaining exposed and easy targets for too long*". On the mine and booby trap range platoons were rotated. One would lay a field of anti-tank and anti-personnel dummy mines detonating thunder flashes for effect, and a second platoon would clear it. Gaps were marked with tracing tape and also a single strand of barbed wire strung through the top eyes of long screw pickets set along each side of the gap. "*After a vehicle gap has been made through a minefield, the platoon leader will have a truck driven through the gap to test thoroughness of the clearing. The floor of the driver's compartment will be sandbagged prior to this operation*".

AREA "E"

THE Croyde area was used for a variety of purposes. The entire beach was designated Croyde Yellow II and used for elementary small practice landings and DUKW exercises in ferrying ashore men, artillery, and equipment. Behind the beach among the dunes was a tented encampment for troops under training with their officers billeted in holiday camp chalets at the opposite end of the beach.

Driving in narrow Devon lanes presented real problems for some Americans, especially tank drivers of the 38th Cavalry Reconnaissance Squadron who were temporarily attached to the Assault Training Centre. On 24th February 1944 Technician Sergeant Robert L. Denny of F Company drove a tank from Georgeham towards Croyde, colliding with a stone wall outside Croyde Stores causing an estimated £10.00's worth of damage. At the subsequent inquiry it was found that Denny was drunk and had taken the tank without authorisation. Just over a month later Technician Fifth Grade Guy M. Elrod of the same company collided with a car driven by a Polish pilot from 304 Squadron, R.A.F. Chivenor.

It wasn't only tank drivers who found difficulty in negotiating lanes around Croyde and Georgeham. A local farmer reported his van was hit on 7th January 1944 by an American jeep driven by T5 Melvin Silvia of L Company, 156th Infantry Regiment, and on 1st March 1944 Private Alvin J Guidry of Cannon Company, 156th Infantry Regiment collided his jeep with a car driven by the Braunton doctor.

Once training had ceased at the Assault Training Centre, the entire site including Croyde camp was taken over by the 197th Replacement

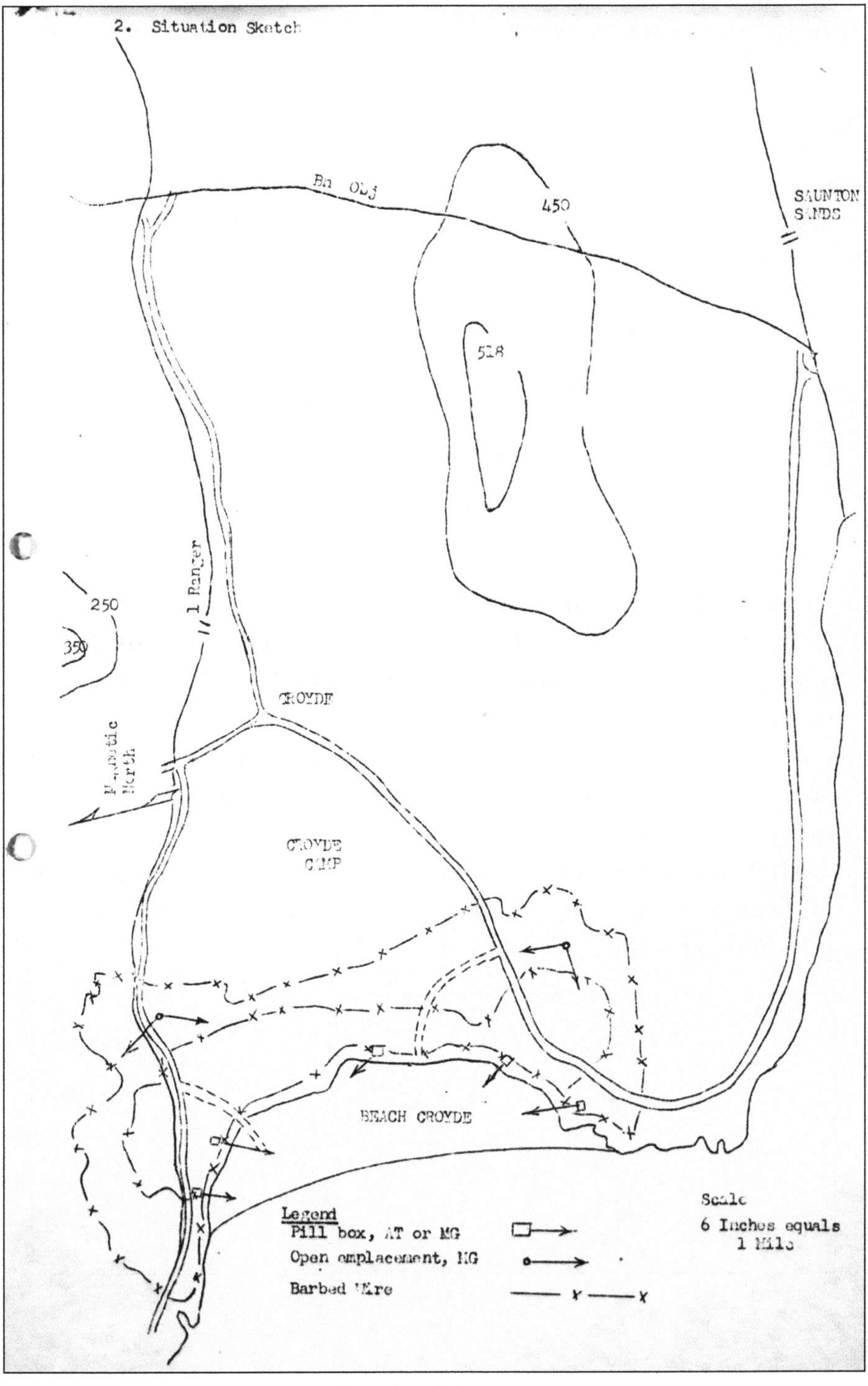

Croyde training area.

Croyde Bay.

Company. On 19th July 1944 the local Coastguard reported that … *"an unknown female bather had been rescued from the sea at Croyde Bay in the afternoon by a coloured American soldier Johnson Private Rudolph of the 197th. Before he had entered the water he handed his gold wrist watch to another female who was missing when he came out"*. Police made enquiries but were unable to trace the female who held the watch or the rescued person.

High spirited American soldiers thought it great fun to bodily lift beach huts from their hard standing and move them to different positions in the line.

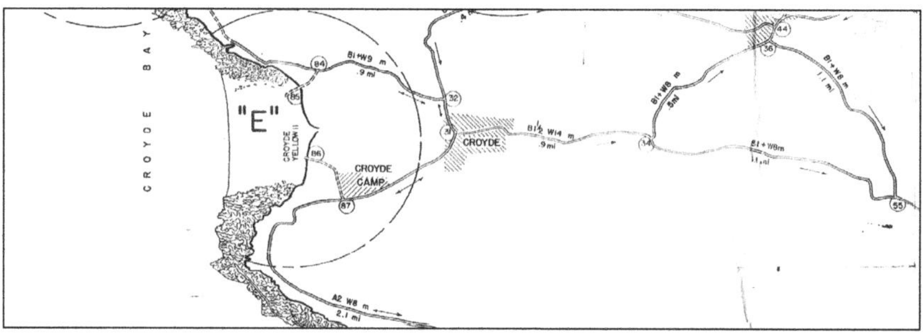

Map.

AREA "F"

BAGGY Point was a late addition to the Assault Training Centre's training areas when a need for Company sized rehearsals was identified. This was noted by the ATC on 25th October 1943 and the highest priority was given to constructing the necessary training aids. Just over two weeks later the ATC Diary Notes ..."*A new type of exercise has been added to our training which is that of the assault company. It was found that there was too great a gap from the training in individual and team assault to the complete battalion exercise. The company exercises are held in the Baggy Point area and live ammunition is used*".

Baggy Point dummy pillbox.

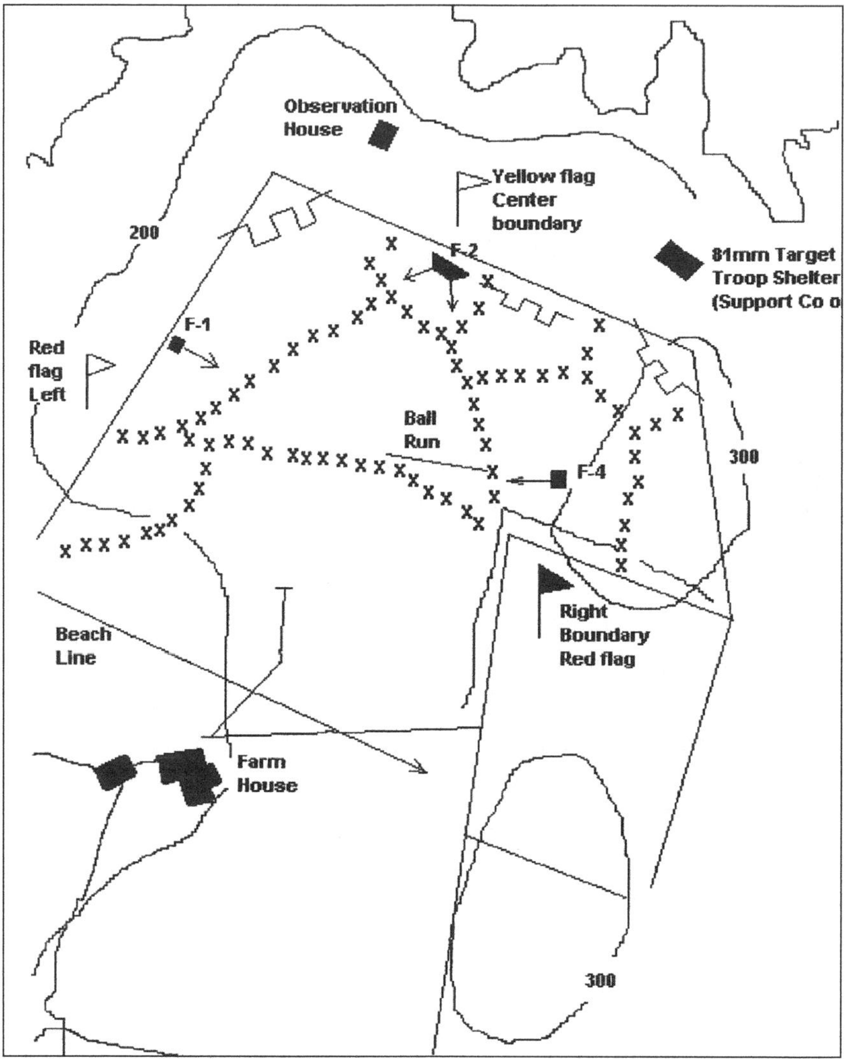

Baggy Point.

To create this new exercise range some of the original farm banks and hedges were removed and the gaps can still be seen today. Three huge concrete blocks representing enemy pillboxes are situated within the boundary hedgeline and behind the main training area are several smaller training "faces". Fingered into the wet concrete of one is the name, A.A. Augustine. His unit was responsible for many of the constructions in the Assault Training Centre, and landed ahead of the infantry on the enemy shore. Private Alfred A. Augustine, Company

B, 146th Engineer Combat Battalion was killed in action on "Omaha" beach on D-Day.

In 1997 the National Trust, headed by Shirley Blaylock, undertook a detailed historic landscape survey, which was published late in 1999. In it the National Trust recognises the significance of these remains by grading them as being of "Regional importance". They admit that … " *three of the structures (6F, 9F and 10F) were destroyed by the National Trust some time ago before there was a recognition that concrete structures from WW II were of historical and archaeological value*", but now recommend that … " *surviving dummy pillboxes and associated earthworks should be retained as features of national interest*".

The Observation House only exists today as a low sandy mound with some mortared brickwork protruding above ground level and the Troop Shelter was never a construction, just a wall of sandbags along the rim of a disused quarry on the cliff top. Ranger battalions tasked with destroying the troop shelter confounded the exercise umpires by taking an unexpected approach across the cliff face from Croyde and took the position from the rear.

Cliff climbing.

As the Rangers proved, there were uses for the cliffs of Baggy Point but the ATC had already noticed them. The Assault Training Center Diary Notes for 22nd October 1943 explains their pioneering work … *"The practice of landing small groups by rubber boats in odd places has been sufficiently successful, to lead, to the attempt to make a much more important factor of it. It is referred to as "Infiltration Landings". In several of the early trials he (Captain Melody) made successful landings on the rocks of Baggy Point. About the first of September 1943, a "raider" section of one officer and 29 men was set up for specialized training in raider tactics and techniques. Subjects stressed were:*

Handling rubber boats, particularly in surf.
Cliff scaling.
Forced marches.
Hand-to-hand combat.
Night operations.

The mission was to land on rocky shores, inaccessible to ordinary craft and establish a small bridgehead. The experiment was so successful that an infantry company is now being trained in these tactics. The ultimate aim is to make this nucleus of a larger group which will land on an unfavorable – hence weakly defended coast, and establish a strong bridgehead which will neutralize enemy coast artillery fire on the assault troops on the beaches. Note that the concept has departed from that of raiding in its usual sense. These forces, to be known as infiltration troops, are not to be hit and run – but to hold on to what they seize till the main force can take over. In this point they resemble airborne units and are in fact, intended to be used in conjunction with them. They carry enough supplies for 48 to 72 hours – counting on resupply over the beaches or by air as the situation permits".

A new exercise had been written by ATC staff, Code A-23 – "Company in the assault of a fortified beach" ..."*the area on Baggy*

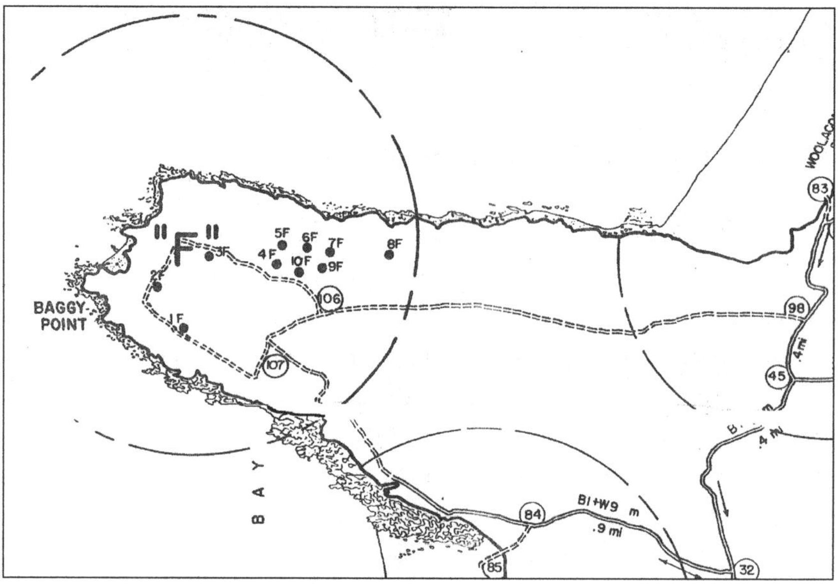

Map.

Point is assumed to be a portion of the German held coast of Northwest Europe. It is part of "Red Beach", which is assumed to be approximately 1200 yards long. The water line is marked on the ground by a line of white and yellow poles. Pillboxes and open emplacements are manned, but enemy reserves have been temporarily immobilized by preparatory bombardment and our paratroops. The strength of the garrison of Red Beach is unknown, but is estimated to be a reinforced platoon.

Your battalion has been ordered to make a daylight landing on Red Beach, assault and overcome the beach defenses and push inland to seize the battalion objective. The battalion is landing with two companies in the assault wave, your company on the left. Four 4.2 inch chemical mortars under battalion control, will lay smoke from H-5 to H Hour.

Your company, with 8 M-4 tanks attached, will assault the beach defenses on its front, seize the beach exit and cover the landing of the support company".

AREA "G"

CODED "Woolacombe Blue" beach below Putsborough was the southernmost of the Woolacombe beaches. It was little used by the Americans except for small-scale landings or specialised cliff-climbing exercises. There was a strongpoint of concrete pillboxes and machine gun posts on the cliffs, and was one of the objectives of larger scale landing exercises further north on Woolacombe Sands.

Debarkation.

AREA "H"

WOOLACOMBE Sands was divided into four beaches. Blue Beach was at Putsborough, and Red Beach was directly in front of the town, between them were Green Beach and Yellow Beach which were the two main destinations for full-scale amphibious assault landings once the troops had learned, practised and mastered their new tactics.

The area of flat sand and scrub immediately behind the beach and below what is now Marine Drive was divided, chequer board style, into small exercise areas, each containing different types of obstacles that engineers and infantry would encounter on the enemy shore and where they learned and practised demolition, mine-laying and mine-removal techniques.

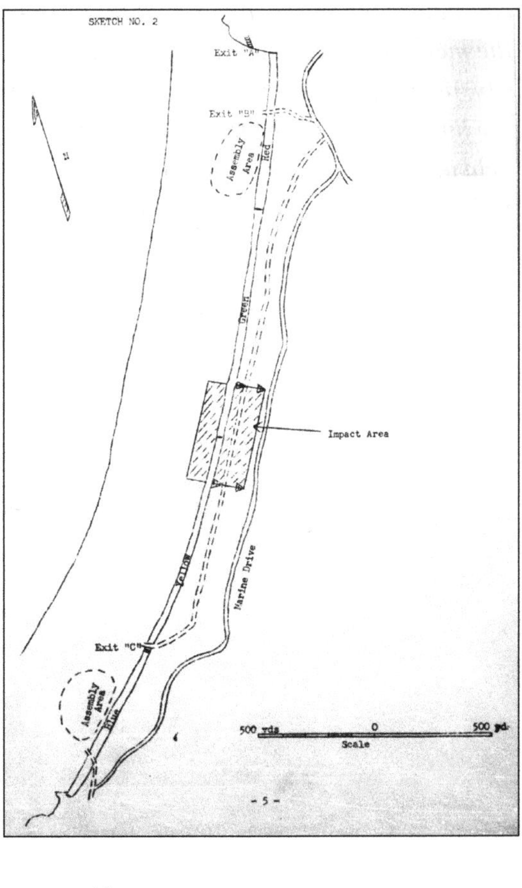

Map.

Time was devoted to the demolition of underwater obstacles and an area was set aside at the southern end of "Blue Beach" below Putsborough. Engineer squads would collect scrap pipe, rail and wooden piling, set them in shallow water, then make up charges, place and fire them. The ATC noted ..."*experiments on passage of underwater obstacles have taken on an increased importance because the Germans have begun to use them to a much greater extent*". While engineers under training continued with routine obstacle demolition lessons and practicals the 1278th and 299th engineers undertook experiments in conjunction with a tank company and some naval elements to produce counter tactics against this new German threat.

Woolacombe Sands saw some of the most intense, large scale military activity of the Assault Training Centre and on Thursday 28th October 1943, Lieutenant Gordon S Ierardi ..."*accompanied and witnessed an assault attack on Woolacombe beach by five infantry companies who landed from DUKWs. Saw the loading and rode with the men into the assault onto the beach. As explained to me by Colonel Ely, the purpose of the attack was to hold the captured bridgehead and the hills back of the beach. The group attacking the left flank were to be held up while the two groups attacking the center and the right flank were to be permitted to reach the top of the hills, which were their objectives.*

Practice landing.

Woolacombe beach.

If the center companies gain the top of their hill and then swing off and encircle the left hill, relieving the left companies who are under fire from the hill, and thus permitting them to advance, the problem is a success and the attackers have won. If the center attackers reach the top of their hill, hold it, and maintain a strong reserve, the problem is considered a draw. If the center attackers achieve the top of their height and then swing away off to the right or continue their advance forward, it is assumed that the whole attacking force would be split and the beachhead lost. The attacking force followed the correct course and the problem was adjudged in their favor. The unit which carried out this exercise was the 2nd Battalion of the 116th Infantry".

This was Field Exercise #1 and assaulting formations were given detailed information in order to plan their attack which, unknown to them, was exactly like the real invasion plan. The attackers were to assume that a Ranger battalion had seized the high ground on their flanks and destroyed fixed guns that threatened their landing. The British forces were to their left, and their landing was to be in daylight. Realism was added too by the presence of School Troops at the "enemy" fortifications – and they had their orders too. They were allowed a generous amount of blank ammunition for machine gun and anti-tank weapons, and instructed to loose off parachute flares in order to confuse signals of the landing force as well as laying trip wires connected to small sticks of explosive in the barbed wire.

The first formal landing exercise had been made on 14th October by "School troops" on Woolacombe sands and it was recorded that …"*Colonel Thompson was the first American to step ashore and the inexperienced troops were judged enthusiastic doing well, and the Navy personnel handled their craft well in the surf conditions*".

On 23rd October 1943 the first landing exercise on Woolacombe beach by a Regimental Combat Team was held and the results were good except for an unexpected shortage of craft. Lieutenant General Gerow, Commanding General of the U.S. V Corps had watched the exercise and wanted more umpiring and the for the Naval Officer in charge to overcome cautious restrictions.

In February 1944 the 16th Regimental Combat Team of the 1st Infantry Division undertook a regimental landing team exercise using the 16th Infantry Regiment; 7th Field Artillery Battalion; Company F 38th Mechanised Cavalry; Company A 803rd Tank Destroyer Battalion; Companies A and B 1st Engineer Battalion; Company A 81st Chemical Battalion; Company B 234th Engineers (as shore party). Their mission was to destroy enemy beach defences and strong points, seize the regimental objective, organise it against hostile counter attack and be prepared for further advance. A defending force was physically represented on the high ground in the vicinity of the battalion objective and at the Putsborough strong point by school troops wearing red hat bands. Blank ammunition and half-charge demolitions were issued with the warning that … "*ammunition will not be fired closer than 20 yards to personnel*" and "*physical contact between members of opposing forces is prohibited*".

AREA "L"

THIS was basically Woolacombe town itself where the Assault Training Centre's headquarters was based in the Woolacombe Bay Hotel, and the town's boarding and private houses played host to many officers. The area included one little used landing beach, "Woolacombe Red" that was too dangerous for amphibious assault landings because of its proximity to the rocks and was used as a buffer zone for craft that were swept off their designated landing spots.

A frequent visitor to North Devon, Mr C. remembers ... "*When in 1947 I first visited Woolacombe I remember seeing a bronze plaque fixed to the wall – now the car park – about 10" by 12". This plaque commemorated 98 U.S. Army personnel who were drowned in Woolacombe Bay whilst preparing for the D-Day landings. To our horror some years later we discovered it was missing, only to think that it had been bulldozed into the ground on enlargement of the car park*".

An eye witness account, perhaps of the same event is given by Mrs H ... "*At the time that training took place for the coming invasion of Europe in 1944, I lived with my mother in Mortehoe and worked in the "Red Barn" café near the beach. I can recall one day helping my mother to give first aid to many who had been recovered from the sea when barges were overturned and sank. The café was used as a rescue station and I can remember the floor being covered with troops needing resuscitation and that many lives were lost that day*".

This incident occurred on 18th December 1943 and the casualties were from 743rd Tank Battalion who lost 7 men and the U.S. Navy lost three sailors. This tragedy is recalled by Major Pixton who ... "*was unable to be on the beach as the initial waves were coming ashore, but was in my office on the third floor of the headquarters hotel, the office facing the beach. I looked out the window to see the waves of landing craft approaching the beach. Off to my right were three landing craft by themselves which were much too far to the north of the beach area and were heading directly for the rocks. The landing craft were LCMs, which were designed for carrying a tank, a truck, a couple of jeeps, or personnel. Each of these three LCMs was carrying a tank. They waited until they were close to the rocks before they took any action. Then as if by command, all three of them turned to their right toward the sandy part of the beach area. By then they were inside the line of breaking waves. The minute I saw them I yelled at an assistant who was in the office to bring me my chest waders immediately. As I was putting them on I was watching the three landing craft and the inevitable happened. Because the surf waves were big that day, and the landing craft were travelling parallel to the waves, all three of them capsized. I ran to the beach to help in any way possible, but there was nothing which could be done at that time. The tide was in and the surf was heavy. We had to wait until the tide receded before we could do anything. There were fourteen men killed that day in that incident, nine soldier tank crewmen and five Navy landing craft crewmen. I personally pulled nine drowned tank crewmen out through the turrets of the three tanks. Lifting that dead weight was extremely difficult. We also had to turn over the*

Capsized craft incident.

upside down landing craft so they could be recovered and removed. That was the most physically exhausting day of my life, as well as the emotional strain which accompanies such incidents. To my knowledge that was the single most costly training accident we ever had at the training center".

The only traceable casualties are :

Ensign Clarence D Briggs Buried Iowa, USA	188691	USNR	KiA
Ensign M J White Commemorated ABMC, Cambridge	0-225819	USNR	MiA
Coxswain Marvin S Simms Buried New Jersey, USA	8172446	USN	KiA
T5 Stanley J Chesney Buried ABMC cemetery, Cambridge	33014011	743 Tk Bn	KiA
Pfc Henry N Jelle Buried ABMC cemetery, Cambridge	37272250	743 Tk Bn	KiA
T4 Marvin Quintanilla Buried ABMC cemetery, Cambridge	38159706	743 Tk Bn	KiA
Pfc Henry O Cox Buried ABMC cemetery, Cambridge	37282990	743 Tk Bn	KiA

Plus seven other Army personnel killed in action.

Overlooking this beach is the Assault Training Centre memorial which was dedicated in May 1992 by Brigadier General Paul W. Thompson. The inscription reads ... *"On the sixth of June 1944 three Allied armies – British, Canadian and American invaded the continent of Europe over the heavily fortified beaches of Normandy – It was the greatest amphibious assault in military history and was a decisive battle of World War II – In the autumn of 1943 the United States Army Assault Training Centre was established at Woolacombe with headquarters in the village and encompassed Woolacombe and Saunton Sands their adjacent hinterlands and the sea approaches – This memorial is dedicated to those thousands*

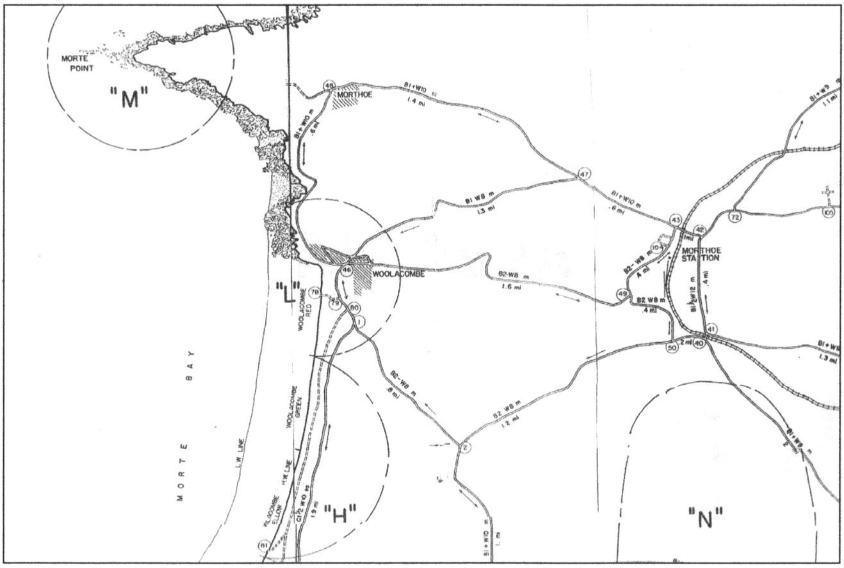

Map.

of American soldiers whose preparation on the sands of Woolacombe and Saunton in the months preceding D-Day carried them to glorious victory on the sands of Normandy."

The Woolacombe Bay Hotel had been requisitioned as the Assault Training Centre's headquarters in 1943 and now shelters a bronze plaque in the entrance lobby to commemorate the American wartime presence. First Lieutenant Robert O. Coll was posted to the U.S. Assault Training Centre to be Assistant Personnel Officer ... *"One night I was Officer of the day, and at about 3.00 am the phone rang. Did I know a Captain Peckham ? Cautiously I said yes. All of our activities were so secret that I hardly knew what to say. Well, the MP, I presume, said that he had been found drowned in one of the enormous water containers, perhaps fifty feet square, that were in London for fire fighting. Obtaining his phone number I awakened Colonel Metheny – Executive Officer, to deliver the message. Was this an accident or sabotage? I never heard any more"*. Another strange and unrecorded happening was witnessed by the same officer when ... *" one evening a small plane, fighter – U.S. I believe, crashed in the sea very close to the pounding waves on the rocky coast, to the west of the beach and lawn in front of the Bay Hotel. I think the pilot was rescued"*.

AREA "M"

MORTE Point formed the most northern practical boundary of the Assault Training Centre and the promontory was used as a target for sea borne artillery cruising off Woolacombe Sands.

Major Russell T. Finn joined the Assault Training Centre staff in early 1943 as head of the artillery section and was almost immediately confronted by the problem of supplementing direct fire onto enemy fortifications as the assault waves closed on the shore. And he came up with an ingenious scheme. He remembers ... "*To the best of my knowledge artillery had never before been fired from landing craft. The ATC experimented with the idea and had a partial solution. The difficulty with firing land based artillery pieces from landing craft is the lack of a stable platform. The two requisites, direction and distance (range) are the same whether on land or sea. The landing craft can be moved in the general direction of the target and the range can be determined with range finders on the craft. The range is normally set on the cannon by means of levelling a bubble. The solution we used was for the range finder operator to continuously call out ranges. The range setter on the weapon would set the ranges and the gunner responsible for firing would watch the range bubble, and when centred, would fire*".

The Assault Training Centre Diary Notes record that ... "*On 21st September 1943 artillery was fired from landing craft for the first time at the Assault Training Center, and for the first time in ETO. Battery "A" 224th F.A. 29th Division furnished the materiel and personnel. The battery was loaded aboard an LCT5 at Crow Point and moved out to the vicinity of Baggy Point. The target range was located on Morte Point. Ranges of 5,000 yards and less were fired*". On 24th January 1944 the Assault Training Centre Diary Notes had to add ..." *In connection with firing weapons from craft it is interesting to note that the artillery officers of the RCT's that come for training are generally very dubious when they hear of it, and are surprised by the successful results*".

The initial experiment had used two types of artillery piece for comparison, towed howitzers and self-propelled guns of the same calibre. The four towed 105mm howitzers were loaded onto an LCT-5 with their prime movers, one ammunition truck and three jeeps. The self-propelled battery was divided with three howitzers on each of two LCT-5s. Chains with turnbuckles were used to secure the howitzers to the craft. Wheeled vehicles were chocked and blocked, and no difficulties were experienced with the howitzers moving due to recoil, nor did any loads shift due to rough seas. Their target on Morte Point was a two hundred yard square subdivided into four one hundred yard squares. Data taken at the time shows that accuracy on the smaller target was between 34 and 45 per cent, and on the larger 200 yard target, accuracy more than doubled, giving Major Finn the optimism to quote that an accuracy of 60 per cent was achievable.

Encouraged by their initial success, and continuing the tradition of the Assault Training Centre of innovation, experiments were conducted in firing the 155mm self-propelled gun from an LCT. The conclusions were that it was as accurate as the smaller 105mm field pieces, but to justify its use in the early waves it would need to hit individual pillboxes, something that could not be guaranteed. The Assault Training Center Diary Notes of 14th November 1943 observed that ... "*Owing to its flat trajectory, "lost overs", when firing on Morte Point were a cause of considerable concern to the range officer*". There is no record of the 155mm gun being used afloat on D-Day.

In December 1943, encouraged by their artillery success, 57mm anti-tank guns were fired from DUKWs but their accuracy was found to be poor, so despite being technically achievable their value was "*highly questionable*".

VISITORS

WITH so many secrets to keep, the Assault Training Centre covered itself with a shroud of official secrecy so successfully that decades later it remains almost impenetrable.

The ATC's mission was so vital to the success of the impending D Day that even the local population really knew very little of what went on, but there were occasions when limited media exposure suited the ATC.

There was already a never ending queue of visitors to the Assault Training Centre from the very day of its opening. Military personnel were professionally intrigued by what was happening here, and it was a showcase of American military might, proudly exhibited on chosen dates, to diplomats, politicians, and military "top brass". But even by 30th September 1943 as the Centre's Diary Notes ... *"Unofficial 'observers' and hangers-on are to be eliminated in future"*. The situation became so intense that the Assault Training Centre took official action as was noted on the 14th October ...*"It has become evident that this organization has become a center of attraction for high ranking officers and officials of both nations. As a result of this and other factors the office of Headquarters commandant was set up, one of its functions being that of Visitors Bureau"*.

Media interest was intense and although the press were made welcome to what was a "secret" establishment, they were closely chaperoned around carefully selected activities as on 31st October 1943 when the Centre ...*"received large (46 in number) delegation of press representatives. Day passed very successfully all representatives agreeing that day was very much worthwhile. They were impressed especially with precise organization of their schedule*".

Then came one of the two most important inspection visits of all. Just about every unit commander of the Allied invasion force was to descend in one party on 19th November 1943. For security reasons they travelled in two separate trains from London. Thompson recalls ... "*A train party of the highest brass, American and British descended on Woolacombe to observe a regimental combat team landing assault operation... practically everyone of note except Lord Louis Mountbatten (we always thought it irked him that Woolacombe had turned out so well for us)*". Their schedule of events opened with a brief introduction to the Assault Training Centre, and then a description of what they would be seeing ..."All *events on today's program are normal training schedule items. Troops concerned are chiefly elements of the 115th RCT of 29th Infantry Division. Troops have been at Center 10 days and will remain 7 days more. First 9 days have been devoted to individual and small-unit training; today's schedule marks start of training on battalion scale. Training period ends with a regimental landing-assault exercise*". The top brass were then escorted around the Assault Training Center in a long, winding convoy of jeeps, and parked finally in Woolacombe to watch an assault landing on Woolacombe Sands.

Between 1st October 1943 and 31st January 1944, which represents most of the Centre's working life, it played host to 805 official visitors.

On 20th and 21st February 1944 another very important party arrived under the code name "Exercise Brandy". This time it was a group of Russian officers who were given the grand tour of the Centre, perhaps as a politically supportive gesture to the British and American promise to Stalin of opening the "Second Front". Witnessing the activities and objectives of the Assault Training centre would hopefully convince the Russians of the sincerity of that promise. Their only recorded Russian comment was ..."*Where are the supporting aircraft?*"

On 12th January 1944 ..."*A group of seven Russian officers headed by Major General A. Sharapov visited the Center with escorts and interpreters. They indicated a keen interest in the activities here, but did not put forth many comments. Their tour of observation went off smoothly*".

U.S. Army Here Blueprint The 'Invasion'

MAN FROM INSIDE WEHRMACHT LEADS

By VICTOR LEWIS, 'Daily Sketch' Special Correspondent, At a U.S. Assault Training Centre, Monday

THE fight for every foot of the first 1,000 yards of the Fortress of Europe by American assault troops has been worked out in detail. Every man who will take part in this vital amphibious operation has been, or is being, trained to a split second in what he will do.

In this "somewhere-in-England" assault centre he is learning hour after hour, under hazardous, realistic conditions, to overcome the obstacles he will meet. This, so far as the American army is concerned, is where the invasion is being hatched.

Beaches Reproduced

Under a man who for years up to the early days of the war studied German army tactics—from inside the German Army—American assault forces are learning each move in what may be one of the greatest battles in history when the first assault forces must break down the heavily fortified beaches of Europe.

Every detail of the beaches has been reproduced with pillbox positions with their interlocking bands of fire, barbed-wire used exactly as the Germans use it, every known German type of tank obstacle, anti-tank and anti-personnel mines, mortars and artillery.

Officers from the landing at Salerno are passing on valuable information. Men are briefed from huge relief

A new tank capable of fording rivers advances over difficult country during the great assault exercise. The purpose of the two objects resembling ventilators on the tank is a military secret.

Daily Sketch – November 1943.

A Press party of 24 correspondents were given a tour of the ATC on 3rd March 1944 including representatives from U.S. newspapers, First U.S. Army Group, and the Daily Mirror. A week later a general tour of the ATC was made by 21 high ranking officers, 6 of them British, and two newspaper correspondents. Just two days later Lieutenant General Hodges, Major General Collins and Colonel van Fleet watched a beach assault, were given a tour of ATC facilities and shown several demonstrations.

On 18th April 1944 a beach assault demonstration was to be given to Major General Barton and Brigadier General Roosevelt of the 4th Infantry Division with Colonels Tally and Matchett of V Corps Engineer Special Brigades but due to bad weather it was cancelled and a conference substituted.

Official visitors

October 1943	=	156
November 1943	=	199
December 1943	=	181
January 1944	=	264
February 1944	=	442
March 1944	=	363
April 1944	=	206

CASUALTIES

CONSIDERING the vast number of troops involved in live-fire exercises, and the realism of battle added by instructors, it is a tribute to the safety rules imposed by the Assault Training Center that the casualty rate for troops under training was not much higher.

Invariably casualties were the result of some unforeseen circumstances or complete accidents. As Lieutenant Ierardi reported that in the week prior to his arrival on 26th October 1943 …"*A most unfortunate accident occurred. While troops were being trained to advance under machine gun fire, one of the guns either went out of control or lost the correct range, firing into a group of men, killing five and wounding fourteen. On Saturdays Hedgehog, another couple were hurt. An inexperienced 57mm gun crew went completely haywire and fired a shot into one of the houses of the little village of Croyde from the training area. In every week there are several casualties, but this is the price which must be paid for this most valuable training*".

On 25th October 1943 Colonel Thompson interviewed the officers and non-commissioned officer involved in the machine gun fatalities, reported his findings to higher headquarters and appointed a board of officers to investigate the accident but his preliminary questioning failed to disclose the cause. Settings on the gun were found to be correct when checked immediately after the accident. The following day Thompson visited Colonel Lee to discuss the accident and it was emphasised to him that "*training must continue and officers must so conduct themselves that there will be no loss of confidence on the part of the men*".

Ierardi continued …"The *training undertaken at the Assault Training Center is taken most seriously and at times is definitely hazardous. Training with live ammunition presents a real problem. The problems (exercises) must be intense enough to acquaint the participating troops with actual battle conditions and indicate to them proper methods of self-defense but on the other hand, they must not be so intense as to frighten the individual soldier and injure his fighting spirit. The Center makes every effort to achieve this goal and I believe that they achieve their aim. However occasional violent accidents are unavoidable*".

There was no accounting for freak accidents such as the sergeant who was killed by a bullet ricocheting off a steel stake supporting barbed wire entanglements during a battalion assault exercise. A mortar exploded killing two of the crew, probably due to a manufacturing defect in the mortar or ammunition, and during a Hedgehog exercise an infantryman was badly injured when a 60mm mortar shell landed short of its target and a fragment of its exploding shell penetrated his thigh.

In an October exercise, a 57mm anti-tank shell fell through the roof of the Saunton Sands Hotel which temporarily housed the Duke of York School evacuated from the dangers of Dover. Colonel Thompson remembers "*jeeping immediately to the scene, being welcomed (?) by the headmaster, being shown the hole in the ceiling through which the projectile had come, being shown how close it had come to where, normally, students would have been sitting – and finally being presented with the projectile itself*".

Thompson also recalls another incident, this time involving a Group Captain Chilton from RAF Chivenor "*I took care to keep the worthy Group Captain advised of our training schedules, and I had impressed upon him that our realism in training included artillery, mortar and anti-tank fire, some of it with high trajectories. This however did not deter him from a sport he relished, going aloft in his little Tiger moth to observe our exercises as from an elevated grandstand seat. It was a Regimental combat team landing assault exercise and I was observing from a knoll, and alongside was the division commander. All at once the general says to me "Thompson, is that part of the exercise ?" I followed his gaze and saw (a) a little Tiger Moth airplane disintegrating, and (b) a parachute beginning to open. Taking time to tell the general, "No, that is not part of the exercise, but I know what it is". I with great reluctance put in train the process for suspending the exercise, we sent a DUKW out in the bay and fished the Group Captain out of the water … As for the Group Captain – as he floated seaward he was observed methodically to divest himself of all clothes except underwear; before shedding his pants, he was observed to extract his wallet, which he was clutching when pulled aboard the DUKW".*

STAFF LIST

ON 6th April 1943 the nucleus of Colonel Thompson's staff was formed as they were officially relieved from their assignments and transferred to the provisional Assault Training Centre. These men had been personally selected by Thompson for the experience and expertise they would bring to the Assault Training Centre in a variety of ways.

Lt Col Myles W. Brewster	017597	
Lt Col Morris T. Warner	01566562	Inf
Capt Chester H. Albright	0369187	Med
Capt Thomas J. Murphy	0320267	Inf
Capt Mac A. Palmer	0401497	Inf
1st Lt Rederick E. Kleeb	0408696	AGD
2nd Lt Lewis E. Beacock Jr	0422336	Inf
2nd Lt James J. Drislane	01578397	QMC
2nd Lt Jonah Kaufman	01578689	QMC
2nd Lt David N. Short	01579109	QMC
1st Sgt Harry Gordon	20714920	
Pvt John J. Karczewski	35170230	
Pvt John T. Doyle	32168519	

Major Allan G. Pixton lectured on the functions and responsibilities of the Engineer Amphibious Brigades who were to establish staging areas and supply dumps on the beaches, process all personnel, vehicles, supplies and equipment across the beachhead area. His specialisation was in great demand for every three weeks he would travel to the

ATC staff.

Joint "Q" Planning School in London, the Anglo-American school for training logistics officers in combined amphibious landings.

Colonel E.P. Lock Jr. had been the Chief of Training at the Engineer School, Fort Belvoir and was seconded to the London doctrine conference before being selected by Thompson as his ATC Chief of Staff.

Chief of the Training Section was Lieutenant Colonel Lucius P. Chase whose maternal grandparents had emigrated to the United States from the Barnstaple area. His expertise and administrative capabilities shone through as he was the driving force in organising the London doctrine conference and was one of the first officers to be selected by Thompson.

Colonel Myles W. Brewster was appointed Chief of the Doctrine Branch being transferred from the U.S. European Theatre of Operations General Staff. After the war he married an English girl and settled in East Anglia.

The ATC's liaison with the combat team commanders was handled by Colonel John Battle Horton as Chief of the Assault Branch and who eventually succeeded Colonel Thompson as the ATC Commandant in early March 1944.

Staff List

Albright Capt Chester H.	0369187	MC	Surgeon, Special Staff
*promoted Major and Chief, Medical Sec, Stn Complement died 1974			
Anderson 1st Lt Charles L.		Inf	Serv Co 156th Inf, Claims Officer
Arnold Capt Robert M.		SC	Signal Section, Assault
Bach Maj Stanley K.		Inf	Infantry Section, Assault
Bailey Capt Joseph S.		Inf	Supporting Section, Amphibious
Bamford Capt Warren H.		CE	Engineer Section, Assault
Baray Capt Robert R.	0-447973	CE	Range Section, Training
* from Service of Supply, Southern Base Section			
Barber 1st Lt Donald P.		Inf	S-1 Section, Station Complement
Barbour 1st Lt Paul H. Jr		MC	Medical Sec, Station Complement
Barysh Maj Noah		MC	Chief, Medical Section, Assault
* promoted to Lt Colonel			
Baxter Lt Col Charles E. Jr		QMC	Chief, Supply & Construction
Bayless Capt William G.		Inf	Chief, Intelligence Section
Beacock 2d Lt Lewis E. Jr	0422326	Inf	
Beatson Capt John B.		GAC	Chief, Anti-Aircraft Section, Trng
Betsen 2nd Lt Casper F.		Inf	Range Section, Training
Boseman Maj William A.		Inf	Tactical Exercises, Assault
Boyle 1st Lt Charles E.		CE	Infiltration Section, Amphibious
Brewster Lt Col Myles W.	017597	GSC	Chief, Doctrine & Development
* promoted Colonel, Chief Redeployment Co-ordinating Group 1945			
Brewster Maj John P.		FA	Artillery Section, Assault
Bright 2nd Lt Eugene W.		FA	Assistant Adjutant, Special Staff
Calhoun Capt Howard O.		Inf	Anti-Tank Co 156th Inf Air Defense
Campagna 2nd Lt Joseph R.		FA	Artillery Section, Assault
Campbell Capt John A.		CE	Engineer Section, Assault
Campbell Capt Laurie P.		Inf	Co A 156th Inf Dep Fire Marshal
Campbell WOJG Bobbie O.		USA	S-4 Section, Station Complement
Cauble Maj Gordon B.		SC	Signal Officer, Special Staff
*promoted to Chief, Signal Section, Assault			
Chaney Capt Edgar L. Jr		Inf	Serv Co 156th Inf, Munitions
Chase Col Lucius P.	0-178374	Inf	Chief, Training
* D-Day Executive Officer 6th Engineer Special Brigade			
Coll 2nd Lt Robert O.		FA	S-1 Section, Station Complement
Culley 1st Lt Charles C.		SC	Chief, Photography Section
Curry Capt Charles L.		CE	Supporting Section, Amphibious
* D-Day – 5th Engr Sp Bde – Asst S-4			
Daigle 1st Lt L. E.		Inf	Attached, Infantry Section, Assault

Dann Capt Daniel I.		MC	Medical Section, Assault
Day Col Alfred C.	0-136537	CWS	Chief, Chmcl Section, Amphibious
* D-Day – Deputy Chief Chemical Warfare Officer			
De Kruyff Lt Col Richard D.		CE	Supporting Section, Amphibious
* D-Day – 6th Engr Sp Bde Provost Marshal			
Dervas 1st Lt James		CE	Engineer Section, Assault
Deutsch Lt Col Albert		Inf	Doctrine & Development
* July 1944 – Omaha Beach Command			
Dobbins Maj S.O.H.		CE	Hq Commandant, Special Staff
Doyle Pvt John T.	3216819		
Drislane 2d Lt James J.	01578397	QMC	
*promoted to 1st Lt and Chief, S-1 Sec, Station Complement			
Echols Capt Eugene S.		CE	Supporting Section, Amphibious
* D-Day XO 131 QM Battalion, later promoted Major			
Elias 2nd Lt Albert J.		CE	Supporting Section, Amphibious
Elliott 1st Lt Frank A.		CE	Infantry Section, Assault
Ely Col Louis B.		FA	Director, Amphibious
* Korean war veteran – Commander Special Activities Group			
Ernest 1st Lt Herbert M.		DC	Medical Sec, Station Complement
Finn Lt Col Russell T.		FA	Chief, Artillery Section, Assault
* XO 32nd FA Battalion as Colonel			
Fakleman 2nd Lt Joseph J.		Inf	Attached, Infantry Section, Assault
Friesz 1st Lt L. O.		Inf	Attached, Infantry Section, Assault
* Oct 1944 – Seine Section as Captain			
Gamble 2nd Lt Julian B.		Inf	Attached, Infantry Section, Assault
Gillan WOJG Patrick J.		USA	Hq Co 156th Inf, Asst Comm
Gillespie Lt Col R.L.		Inf	Chief, Administration
* Oct 1944 – Seine Section as Colonel			
Gordon 1st Sgt Harry	20714920		
Haas Lt Col George A.		Inf	Inspector, Special Staff
Hacker 2nd Lt Alex A.		CE	Infantry Section, Assault
Hackett Maj A. J.		FA	Artillery Section, Assault
Hall Capt DeWitt N.		Inf	Chief, Range Section, Training
Hawkins 1st Lt Malcolm		Inf	Assault Section, Amphibious
Heikkila Capt Frank E.		SC	Signal Section, Assault
* promoted to Major at ATC; 6th Engr Sp Bde Signal Officer as Lt Colonel			
Heywood Capt Alba S.		Inf	S-2, School Troops
Holliday Maj Joseph A.		Inf	S-4, School Troops
Hoppough 2nd Lt Robert L.		NHB	Asst, S-1 Sec, Station Complement
Horton Col John B.		FA	Director, Assault
* Succeeded Thompson as ATC Commandant			
Hoskin 2nd Lt Richard K.		SC	Signal Section, Assault
Houston Lt Col Earl P.		CE	Chief, Supporting Section, Amph
*D-Day – Colonel, 1st Engineer Special Brigade			

Hubbard 2nd Lt L. V.		Inf	Infiltration Section, Amphibious
Hunter Capt Robert F.		CE	Supply & Construction
* D-Day – Asst Commanding Officer 336th Engr Combat Battalion			
Jobes Maj James G.		CE	XO, Supply & Construction
Karczewski Pvt John J.	35170230		
Kaufman 2d Lt Jonah	01578689	QMC	
Kelley 1st Lt Russell J.		Inf	S-4 Sec, Stn Cmplment
*kia 27th July 1944 with 23rd Inf Regt, buried Colleville			
Kennedy Maj Charles E.	0286458	CE	XO, Doctrine & Development
King 1st Lt Samuel C.		CMP	Provost Marshal, Special Staff
Kleeb 1st Lt Roderick E.	0408696	AGD	
Kunzig Lt Col William B.		Inf	Chief, Tactical Exercises, Assault
* May 44 – First US Army			
La Iacona 1st Lt Salvatore		Inf	Assault Section, Amphibious
Lard 1st Lt Arthur D.		Inf	S-4 Section, Station Complement
*promoted to Captain, Co A, 156th Infantry Regiment			
Laycock 2nd Lt R. A.		Inf	Infiltration Section, Amphibious
Learnard Lt Col Henry G. Jr		Inf	Tactical Exercises, Assault
Lewis 2nd Lt Joseph A.		CE	Infantry Section, Assault
Lock Col E.P. Jr		CE	Chief, Operations
* Oct 1944 – Seine Section			
Ludlow 1st Lt Kenneth C.		Inf	Attached, Infantry Section, Assault
Mango Maj Albert E.		MC	Medical Sec, Station Complement
Mathewson 1st Lt John I.		Cav	Infiltration Section, Amphibious
*Kia 28th April 1944 on Exercise Tiger			
Maxfield Capt Alcee F.		Inf	Chief, S-2 & S-3 Sec, Stn Complement
McCaleb Lt Col Albert F.		Inf	Special Services Officer
McCrackin Capt Edward D.	0341543	CE	Infantry Section, Assault
*D-Day 5th Engr Sp Bde as Major			
McKenna Capt R. A.		FA	Artillery Section, Assault
McWhorter Maj William H.		AC	Chief, Air Section, Assault
*departed ATC 19th October 1943			
Melody Capt Philip E.		CE	Chief, Infiltration Section, Amp
Metheny Lt Col L.C.		FA	Executive Officer, Operations
Miller Capt Marcel V.		TC	Supply & Construction
Miller Lt Col H. A.		FA	Executive Officer, Training
Moore Maj Elzie K.		Inf	Chief, Infantry Section, Assault
*D-Day 1st Engineer Special Brigade as Colonel			
Moore 2nd Lt William J.		CE	Infantry Section, Assault
Morrison 2nd Lt Eugene L.		Inf	Attached, Infantry Section, Assault
Murphy Capt Thomas J.	0320267	Inf	
*promoted to Major and Chief, Tank Section, Assault			
Murphy Capt Thomas E.		CE	Supply & Construction
Nachand 2nd Lt E. Garland		Inf	Attached, Infantry Section, Assault
*kia 13th June 1944 with 8th Inf Regt, buried Colleville			

Nowak 1st Lt Charles E.		Inf	Hq Co 156th Inf,Comm Officer
Olin 2nd Lt Harold G.		Inf	Assistant Hq Commandant
* D-Day Lieutenant Medical			
Page Maj Reginald J.B.		CE	Chief, Engineer Section, Assault
*Jun 1945 Lt Col, 463rd AAF Base Unit			
Palmer Capt Mac A.	0401497	Inf	
*promoted to Major, Supporting Section, Amphibious. D-Day 5th Engr Sp Bde			
Petty Capt Frank E.		Inf	Assistant Special Services Officer
Pewinski 2nd Lt F. P.		Inf	Attached, Infantry Section, Assault
Pixton Maj Allan G.		FA	Executive Officer, Amphibious
* 5th Engr Sp Bde as Lt Col			
Pointer Capt Jesse C.		FA	Artillery Section, Assault
Raymond 1st Lt James I.		FA	Chief, Library & Historian
* 1945 Transportation Corps, Engineering Officer as Captain			
Riley 1st Lt Edwin H.		Inf	Navy Liaison Section, Amphibious
Ritchey Capt Dan A. Jr		Inf	Adjutant, School Troops
Robbins 1st Lt Alex		Inf	S-4 Section, Station Complement
Roten Capt Charles T.		Inf	Doctrine & Development
Sargent 2nd Lt Donald		CE	Range Section, Training
Sawyer 1st Lt L. F.		FA	Artillery Section, Assault
Schattenburg Maj Gus A.		Cav	Supply & Construction
Schoenbeck 1st Lt Earle C.		Cav	Supply & Construction
* Sep 1944 Omaha Beach Command as Captain			
Schneider 2nd Lt H.F.		Inf	Range Section, Training
Seawell 1st Lt Walter W.		SC	Signal Section, Assault
Shock 2nd Lt Hobert E.		Inf	Attached, Infantry Section, Assault
Short 2d Lt David M.	01579109	QMC	
*promoted to 1st Lt and X O, Station Complement			
Sibert 1st Lt Ray S.		Inf	Transportation Section
Siverson Lt Col A. G.			Chief, Navy Liaison Section, Amphibious
* Mar 1945 – Cherbourg Port Control			
Smith Capt A. T.		Inf	Tactical Exercises, Assault
Smith 1st Lt B.P.		Inf	Training
Smith 2nd Lt Elmore R.		CE	Navy Liaison Section, Amphibious
Smith Capt Spencer D.		PC	Finance Officer, Special Staff
Smith Maj Stanley K.	0300038	Inf	C O, Station Complement
* Jul 1944 – Omaha Beach Command as Lt Colonel			
Smith 1st Lt Stephen J.		Inf	Chief, Transportation Section
Smith 1st Lt Victor J.		Inf	Chief, S-4 Sec, Station Complement
Stahl 2nd Lt John		AGD	553rd APO Unit, Postal Officer
Stangler 1st Lt Harvey E.		Inf	Co A 156th Inf EM Mess Officer
Stephens Maj Ralph		Inf	Training
Stevens 1st Lt Charles H.		Inf	Co A 156th Inf Off Mess Officer
Swan Capt Casimir J.		SC	Signal Section, Assault
Switzer Maj Frank C.		Inf	S-3, School Troops

Taber 1st Lt Charles S.		AG	Library
Thompson Lt Col Paul W.	017506	CE	Commandant
*wia 6th June 1944 Omaha Beach			
Thompson WOJG Kendrick F.		USA	Transportation Section
Thorn 1st Lt Isaac. W.		Inf	Administration Officer, Amphibious
Tuttle 2nd Lt Richard P.		Inf	S-4 Section, Station Complement
Vaughan 1st Lt Earl D.			Chaplain, Special Staff
Warner Lt Col Morris T.	016562	Inf	
*promoted to Col and C O, School Troops			
Watkins 1st Lt James M.		Inf	Administration Officer, Assault
*KiA 5 Mar 1945 Captain 320th Inf Regt, 35th Inf Div – buried Margraten, Netherlands			
Westerman Maj Harry K.		AGD	Adjutant, Special Staff
Wilkerson 2nd Lt Eugene L.		Inf	Attached, Infantry Section, Assault
Wolf Maj Edwin J.		CE	Chief, Assault Section, Amphibious
* D-Day 6th Engineer Special Brigade – wounded & ordered off the beach			

The majority of staff posts were permanent at the Assault Training Centre, although some junior posts were filled on rotation by officers from combat divisions. When the Centre began to wind down from March 1944 onwards, many officers requested postings to active combat units, or were simply re-assigned as their post was no longer relevant or required. Colonel Finn left for an artillery brigade. Colonel Pixton left in April to join the 5th Engineer Special Brigade and landed on "Omaha" beach at noon of D Day. Major Page moved to U.S. First Army headquarters in Bristol and returned to the United States from Belgium in December 1944.

On 18th January 1944 Colonel Thompson was transferred to First U.S. Army and given command of the 6th Engineer Special Brigade which was to play such an important role in the first vital hours of the "Omaha" landings. He took advantage of the ATC's training facilities by sending about 1,600 men of his new command to exercise in unloading freighters, establishing dumps, clearing the beaches of obstacles and mines, and the construction of beach exits. He always considered this training was of great benefit, particularly following the collapse of the American "Mulberry harbour" when these same units moved more tonnage across the open beaches than the peacetime port of Cherbourg.

Thompson was awarded the "Legion of Merit" for his services in establishing and directing the Assault Training Centre. And was

Paul Thompson

Thompson at desk.

replaced on 7th March 1944 by Colonel John B. Horton who had already lost ..."*twenty seven of the key personnel, and this trend continued to an even greater degree in the last months. They were taken in spite of requests and protests as the work continues in full force and with many new problems due to the specialised nature of the units being trained*". By 20th April 1944 Colonel Horton's biggest problems were turning in supplies and equipment and placing personnel in new assignments. About the same time he estimated that the training area and buildings should be ready to be turned over to the 18th Field Force Replacement Depot by 1st May.

A study of the Assault Training Centre concluded ..."*So we have come to the end of this, and, as Colonel Thompson put it, the success or shortcomings of our work will only show up on the first few thousand yards inland from the beaches of Europe".*

Thompson arrived on "Omaha" beach at H plus 140 minutes and found his engineers pinned down by devastating fire from German fortifications and snipers. Identifying the most prominent enemy emplacement he quickly organised an ad hoc infantry Assault Team from men of various units around him and led the attack. It was successful but Thompson wasn't seen again until the early afternoon when he was found, severely wounded, laying in the draw below the gutted and still smoking German casemate.

UNITS

MANY units of the U.S. Army, Navy and Air Force were involved with the Assault Training Centre, either being trained, training others, or supporting the everyday activities of the Centre.

1st FIGHTER GROUP USAAF

Sep 43 – Participated in Hedge Hog exercise at Assault Training Centre with 175th Regimental Combat Team using 3 Medium bombers & 6 attack aircraft.

1st INFANTRY DIVISION "BIG RED ONE"

08 Feb 44 – 16th RCT took amphibious training to 26th Feb.

24 Feb 44 – 2nd Bn, 18th Inf Regt took amphibious training to 29th Feb.

15 Mar 44 – 3rd Bn, 18th Inf plus one platoon Cannon Company took amphibious training to 20th March.

4th INFANTRY DIVISION "IVY DIVISION"

25 Feb 44 – Movement Order #1. Hq 4th Infantry Div, APO 4, 25 Feb 1944 *"to participate in assault training for the period 1-15 Mar 1944, at the United States Assault Training Center, Woolacombe, England."*

UNIT	OFFICERS	WARRANT OFFICERS	ENLISTED MEN
8th Infantry Regiment (less 3d Bn & Bn Med Sec)	127	6	2525
Det, 12th Infantry Regiment	26	0	120
3d Bn & Bn Med Sec., 22d Inf	43	0	988
Det, 22nd Infantry Regiment	20	0	83
29th Field Artillery Battalion	36	2	570
Det, 42 Field Artillery Battalion	3	0	2
Det, 44 Field Artillery Battalion	3	0	2
Det, 20 Field Artillery Battalion	1	0	1
Co A, 4 Engineer Combat Battalion	7	0	194
Det, Co B, 4 Engineer Combat Bn	1	0	6
Co C, 4 Engineer Combat Bn	6	0	196
Det, 4 Signal Company	1	0	20
Det, 4 Medical Battalion	1	0	0
Co A, 4 Medical Battalion	6	0	112
Det, Co B, 4th Med Bn	3	0	3
Det, Co C, 4th Med Bn	3	0	3
Det, Adj Gen's Sec, Hq 4th Inf Div	1	0	4

11 Apr 44 – Movement Order #8. Cos A and C, 0237 Engineer Combat Battalion, report at the USATC, prior to 12 Apr 44, and upon completion of this temporary duty on or about 19 April 1944.

22 Apr 44 – Movement Order #10. A detachment of the 4th Inf Div, and attached unit, consisting of the number of personnel from units as indicated below:

70 Tank Battalion	2 O	24 EM
Co A, 4 Engineer Combat Battalion	3	
Co B, ..	3	
Co C, ..	3	

Riley 1 Lt Benjamin J 01011260, Inf, 70th Tk Bn, is designated as detachment commander.

5th RANGER BATTALION

Mar 44 – Arrived in UK. To Scotland, Braunton, Devon, Swanage, Dorset for training.

May 44 – *"A group from the 2nd and 5th Ranger Battalions underwent a training period here of three and a half weeks, apparently slightly longer than was planned. Part of this was special purpose or rehearsal work. As the Assault Training Center is not involved in the higher levels of planning, it was necessary for the Rangers to tell us what they had to do and what was needed. All received the same individual training as the Regimental Combat Team 's but their team, company, and battalion exercises were modified as required. Like the Airborne troops, the Rangers were full of enthusiasm and were very proficient with their weapons. They were not as methodical and serious as some other units we have had and there was a tendency to horseplay. Their attitude resulted in improvising and opportunism, but this is fitting for the type of unit and they were alert and keen".*

6th ENGINEER SPECIAL BRIGADE

May 44 – *"Thompson Colonel Paul W, the former Commanding Officer of the Center, conducted two exercises for groups of about 1,600 each. These consisted in landing, establishment of dumps, clearing beaches, construction of exits, etc. They did not involve any instruction by our staff, only the assignment of the areas and such incidental assistance as could be rendered. The units involved needed the opportunity for this sort of practice and the benefit should be correspondingly great. Their training in field sanitation and police had left much to be desired. The problems were well run and were favored by excellent weather."*

8th FINANCE DISBURSING SECTION

ATC Station Complement

03 Nov 43 - At ATC with 2 Officers, 1 WO and 17 EM.

8th INFANTRY REGIMENT

4th Infantry Division

01 Mar 44 – Regiment less 3rd Bn and Med – 127 Off, 6 WO, 2526 EM attended ATC for assault training.

16th INFANTRY REGIMENT

1st Infantry Division

08 Feb 44 – 16th RCT amphibious training at ATC until 26 Feb 44.

18th FIELD FORCE REPLACEMENT DEPOT

01 May 44 – Assault Training Centre closed and handed over to this unit.

18th INFANTRY REGIMENT

1st Infantry Division

24 Feb 44 – 2nd Bn to ATC for amphibious training until 29 Feb 44

15 Mar 44 – 3rd Bn plus one platoon Cannon Co to ATC for training

21st WEATHER SQUADRON

ATC Station Complement

03 Nov 43 – Det based at Woolacombe, Devon with 3 officers and 13 EM.

22nd INFANTRY REGIMENT

4th Infantry Division

01 Mar 44 – 3d Bn and Bn Med Sec of 43 Off, 988 EM attended ATC for amphibious training.

– Detachment of 20 Off, 83 EM attended ATC for training.

28th INFANTRY DIVISION "Keystone"

6 Nov 43 – Advance cadre at ATC

29th FIELD ARTILLERY BATTALION

4th Infantry Division

01 Mar 44 – 36 Off, 570 EM attended ATC for training until 15 Mar 44.

29th INFANTRY DIVISION

Dec 43 – Completed training at ATC. Entire Division participated in concentration and processing for embarkation on Exercise Duck

38th CAVALRY RECONNAISSANCE SQUADRON

10 Feb 44 – As part of 102nd Cavalry Group (Mecz), 2 tank platoons, 1 less tanks, and a troop of Hq attached to ATC until about 06 Mar 44.

40th MOBILE COMMUNICATION SQUADRON

ATC Station Complement

03 Nov 43 – Det M at ATC, based at Woolacombe, Devon with 8 EM.

42nd FIELD ARTILLERY BATTALION

4th Infantry Division

01 Mar 44 – Det of 3 Officers and 3 EM attended ATC for amphibious training until 15 Mar 44.

44th FIELD ARTILLERY BATTALION

4th Infantry Division

01 Mar 44 – Det 3 Off 2 EM attended ATC

70th TANK BATTALION

23 Apr 44 – Attached to 0004 Infantry Division, attended ATC with 2 officers and 24 EM plus detachment

of 4 Engineer Combat Battalion. Designated detachment commander Riley.

81st CHEMICAL BATTALION (MOTORIZED)

ATC Station Complement

03 Nov 43 – Company D at ATC as part of School Troops, based at Lincombe, Devon with 6 officers and 197 EM.

16 Mar 44 – Ltr. Hq V Corps. Subject: Troop Movement. 16 March 1944. To: CO, 81st Chemical Bn (Mtz). "Co B, 81st Chemical Bn (Mtz) to be moved on or about 18 March 1944 for the purpose of participating in a period of combined training with 116th Regimental Combat Team, ending about 30 March 1944.

13 Apr 44 – Ltr. Hq V Corps. Subject: Troop Movement, 13 Apr 1944. To: CO, 81st Cml Bn, Mtz. "1st Plat, Co B, 81st Cml Bn, Mtz. To be moved from present location to Croyde, Devon on 13 April 1944, and attached to Aslt Tng Cen. Upon completion of this training this platoon will return to home station.

101st AIRBORNE DIVISION "SCREAMING EAGLES"

Apr 44 – *"Two groups of about 1000 men each attended ATC each received five days training in April. They were made up of composite units so that companies spread throughout the division would be trained. Again both the staff and the 101st felt it was valuable and regretted that more of them were not able to be in on it. Their assault training did not include dropping or landing by glider and of course no amphibious work. It assumed they had reached the area of their objective and started from that point. They did not use the 30 man assault team (based on the capacity of the LCVP), but proposed teams of parachute infantry platoons consisting of two officers and 35 men and glider infantry platoons of one officer and 46 men. A special area was turned over to them for their final assault problem and this was in the nature of a rehearsal. They showed exceptional energy and enthusiasm*".

109th INFANTRY REGIMENT

28th Infantry Division

Nov 43 – 109th Regimental Combat Team trained at ATC

102nd CAVALRY GROUP (MECHANIZED)

04 Feb 44 – Ltr. Hq V Corps. Subject: Troop movement. 4 Feb 1944. To: CO, 102nd Cavalry Group (Mecz) - to move on or about 10 February 1944. Two (2) Tank Platoons (1)(less tanks) and a Troop headquarters of the 0038 Cavalry Reconnaissance Squadron. One (1) 75mm Assault Gun Platoon with two (2) guns. To be attached until approximately 6 March 1944.

112th ENGINEER COMBAT BATTALION

17 Mar 44 – Ltr Hq V Corps. Subject: Troop Movement. 17 Mar 1944. To: CO, 112th Engr (C) Bn. Co C, 112th Engr (C) Bn to be moved on 18 March 1944. This unit will be attached to 0116 Infantry Regiment for training only.

115th REGIMENTAL COMBAT TEAM

29th Infantry Division

05 Nov 43 – Daily arrival and departure Reports, USATC, 5 Nov 1943.

115th RCT (29th Inf Div)
115th Infantry
110 Field Artillery Battalion
Co's A & C, 0121 Engineer Combat Battalion
Det A, MP Pln, 29th Inf
Det 29 Signal Company

116th INFANTRY REGIMENT

29th Infantry Division

01 Sep 43 – Arrived at ATC for training

Mar 44 – Refresher course at ATC

116th REGIMENTAL COMBAT TEAM

20 Mar 44 – "The 116th Regimental Combat Team returned for a refresher course during 20-29 Mar 44.

This was the only unit to come back for a repetition of the Center's training and several interesting points were noted. They had kept in touch with our changes in technique and after thorough practice and numerous exercises engaged in during the winter, they felt that practically no variations were needed or desirable. The landing exercises were planned by them to be in the nature of rehearsals, and to that extent differed from previous instruction here. The weather permitted all to be made outside the estuary and the problems were very good. Both the RCT and the staff here considered them entirely worthwhile. The improvement shown by the troops in those things they had done in October was obvious and encouraging. Though the organization was slightly modified there was no change in the 30 man boat team.

121st ENGINEER COMBAT BATTALION

29th Infantry Division

Sep 43 – Assault Training Centre for training.

146th ENGINEER COMBAT BATTALION

ATC Station Complement & under training

17 Oct 43 – Assigned to First U.S. Army, APO 230, upon arrival in Britain. To Lincombe Camp, Ilfracombe, North Devon.

27 Oct 43 – Moved to the area of Saunton Sands beach to maintain an assault obstacle course.

05 Nov 43 – Attached to U.S. Assault Training Center, Woolacombe, Devon, England until 4th April 1944. The Battalion's function at Braunton was the maintenance and erection of various courses and ranges for the United States Assault Training Center. This involved work at Woolacombe, Woolacombe Sands, Saunton Sands, Braunton Burrows, and Baggy Point. In connection with the work, allocation of heavy equipment to the Battalion was made necessary. The Battalion operated rock quarries and water points as well as helping to institute and maintain utilities service at Braunton Camp. The Battalion earned an enviable reputation for efficient work and members were commended on various occasions by Colonel Thompson, ATC CO.

04 Apr 44 – Attached to 1121st Engineer Combat Group being deactivated about 01 Apr 44, the 146 ECB was attached shortly thereafter by Army Headquarters to V Corps and subsequently attached to the 1121 ECG at Newquay, Cornwall, England ... for training necessities.

13 Apr 44 – Due to the exigencies of the situation, V Corps recalled the Battalion – first only Company A and then shortly after, the entire Battalion – to Braunton Camp and the former ATC training sites for intensive training for a specialised operation – the clearance of underwater and beach obstacles to aid the Allied assault upon the European mainland.

24 Apr 44 – Company B and Company C arrived at Braunton. H & S Company arrived three days later.

14 May 44 – Letter, Headquarters V Corps. Subject: Troop movement. To: Commanding Officer, 146th Engineer (C) Battalion. Movement from ATC.

146th Engineer (C) Bn. Detachment, 127 vehicles and 236 enlisted men (build-up and residual elements, from USATC to Newquay on or about 14 May 1944. Permanent change of station.

156th INFANTRY REGIMENT

ATC Station Complement

Oct 43 – Regiment, less Detachment attached to ATC as "School Troops"

03 Nov 43 – Assault Training Centre – Woolacombe, Devon.

Unit	Location	Off	WO	EM
Hq Station Complement				
Hq Co, 156th Infantry (less)	Woolacombe	3	1	113
Service Co, 156th Infantry (less)	..	5	2	95
Det A, Co D, 156th Infantry	..	0	0	18
Det A, Med Det, 156th Infantry	..	2	0	21
Anti-Tank Co, 156th Infantry (less)	..	4	0	36
Co A, 156th Infantry	..	7	0	174
Hq & Hq Co, 3rd Bn, 156th Inf (less)	..	2	0	94
Hq School Troops				
Det A, Hq, 156th Infantry	Ilfracombe	18	2	24
Co D, 156th Infantry (less)	Saunton Sands	6	0	149
Co L, 156th Infantry	..	6	0	102
Med Dept Det (less)	Ilfracombe	8	0	60
Hq & Hq Co, 2nd Bn, 156th Infantry	..	8	0	98
Det A, Hq Co, 3rd Bn, 156th Inf	..	1	0	33
Co E, 2nd Bn, 156th Infantry	..	6	0	188
Co F, 2nd Bn, 156th Infantry	..	6	0	186
Co G, 2nd Bn, 156th Infantry	..	6	0	190
Co H, 2nd Bn, 156th Infantry	..	5	0	160

Dec 43 – FUSA Periodic Report, 11 Jan 44 for Dec 43. "156th Inf Regt and 234 Engineer Combat Battalion atchd as school troops conducted assault training for the following units:

Special troops, 29 Infantry Division
112 Engineer Combat Battalion
109 Regimental Combat Team
110 Regimental Combat Team
Officer cadre from 1 Infantry Division and 9 Infantry Division
Btry A, 771 Tank Destroyer Battalion
112 Regimental Combat Team
Co A, 0743 Tank Battalion
Co C & Co B, 0081 Chemical Battalion

162nd SIGNAL PHOTOGRAPHIC COMPANY

ATC Station Complement

03 Nov 43 – Assault Training Centre – Woolacombe, Devon. Det G with 1 Officer and 6 EM.

197th QM GAS SUPPLY COMPANY

ATC Station Complement

03 Nov 43 – 2 officers and 72 EM located at Ilfracombe, Devon

197th REPLACEMENT COMPANY

50th Replacement Battalion

07 Aug 44 – Mrs J.R.W. Shepherd Standing, Pinkney Green, Berkshire, temporary home at Home House, Croyde, age 44, married woman. Reports Kodak folding camera No A118 in brown leather case and two pairs of bathing trunks stolen from a locked beach hut on Croyde Burrows between 6.30 pm 6.8.44 and 11 am 7.8.44. US Army personnel suspected. Enquiries made by US Army CID agents. Camera found in possession of Pvt , 197 Replacement Company, APO 872 stationed at Croyde.

200th FIELD ARTILLERY BATTALION

Dec 43 – FUSA Periodic Report for Dec 43. "received training at ATC.

203rd MP COMPANY

ATC Station Complement

03 Nov 43 – 2 Traffic Platoon at ATC, based at Croyde, Devon with 1 officer and 55 enlisted men.

206th ENGINEERS

30 Apr 44 – Report of A.B.T. Sub-Postmaster of Georgeham Post Office of damage to TK at Georgeham, Devon 10.15 pm by American service personnel. Leather holding straps torn from rivets on door and spring forced from fittings. Men responsible Sgt, A Company 206 Engineers, APO 230; Sfc, USN, Scouts and Raiders, US Navy.

234th ENGINEER COMBAT BATTALION

ATC Station Complement

03 Nov 43 – Based at Ilfracombe, Devon with 28 officers, 3 Warrant Officers and 627 enlisted men.

13 Dec 43 – FUSA Periodic report for Nov 43. "Detail as school troops at the ATC allows no time for unit training"

256th SIGNAL CONSTRUCTION COMPANY

ATC Station Complement

03 Nov 43 – Based at Croyde, Devon with 1 officer and 30 enlisted men.

299th ENGINEER COMBAT BATTALION

14 May 44 – Letter. Hq V Corps, Subject: Troop movement, 14 May
1944. To: CO, 299th Engineer (C) Bn. "299th Engineer (C) Battalion Detachment, 237 enlisted men (build-up and residual elements) from USATC to Paneswick Manor Camp on or about 14 May 1944.

313th FIELD HOSPITAL

31 Jul 44 – Body of 2 Lt J.B. attached to 45 Replacement Battalion US Army, Braunton, Devon found on Saunton Sands approx 8.30 am. Deceased had been bathing at Saunton Sands on 30 Jul 44 with other officers but had not been reported as missing. Body identified by 2nd Lt Alexander E Woodside of same unit. Body removed to Braunton mortuary and later to 313 American Field Station Hospital at Fremington, Devon. Buried at Cambridge American Cemetery.

363rd QM SERVICE COMPANY

ATC Station Complement

03 Nov 43 – Based at Ilfracombe, Devon with 48 EM.

398th ENGINEER GENERAL SERVICE REGIMENT

Aug 43 – Companies C and E were located one and two miles, respectively, west of Braunton. Company D established itself one mile north of Bideford. Company F set up camp a half mile south of Croyde. And Second Battalion Headquarters operated from Saunton Sands.

453rd AMPHIBIOUS TRUCK COMPANY

ATC Station Complement

03 Nov 43 – Based at Croyde, Devon with 7 officers and 175 EM.

07 Dec 43 – 21 personnel, 57 vehicles assigned to 5 Engineer Special Brigade under 131 QM Mobile Battalion.

460th ANTI AIRCRAFT ARTILLERY AUTOMATIC WEAPONS BATTALION

28 Mar 44 – Ltr. Hq V Corps. Subject: Troop movement. To: CO, 460th AAA AW Bn. "To be moved on 29 Mar 1944 for training".

507th MP BATTALION

ATC Station Complement

13 Apr 44 – Ltr. Hq V Corps. Subject: Troop Movement. 13 Apr 1944.
To: CO, Co A, 507th MP Bn. "Movement from ATC. 1st Pln, Co A, 507th MP Bn. To be moved from Woolacombe, Devon to Norton Manor Camp by 22 Apr 1944. This detachment is relieved from temporary duty with U.S. Assault Training Center effective 210001B, April 1944. Permanent change of station.

509th MP BATTALION

ATC Station Complement

03 Nov 43 – 3 Platoon, Company C based at Woolacombe, Devon with 1 officer and 57 EM

553rd ARMY POSTAL UNIT

ATC Station Complement

03 Nov 43 – Based at Woolacombe, Devon with 1 officer and 11 Enlisted Men

634th ANTI AIRCRAFT (AUTOMATIC WEAPONS) BATTALION

ATC Station Complement

03 Nov 43 – Battery "D"

745th TANK BATTALION

ATC Station Complement

03 Nov 43 – Based at Croyde, Devon with 5 officers and 141 EM

802nd SIGNAL SERVICE BATTALION

ATC Station Complement

03 Nov 43 – Detachment based at Woolacombe, Devon with 2 EM

810th SIGNAL SERVICE BATTALION

ATC Station Complement

03 Nov 43 – Detachment based at Woolacombe, Devon with 4 EM

3409th ORDNANCE MEDIUM AUTOMOTIVE MAINTENANCE COMPANY

03 Nov 43 – At ATC Woolacombe, Devon with 4 officers and 116 EM

3422nd ORDNANCE MEDIUM AUTOMOTIVE MAINTENANCE COMPANY

ATC Station Complement

03 Nov 43 – Based at Ilfracombe, Devon with 4 officers and 116 EM

Troops for training usually arrived by train at Braunton railway station where the trains would have to pull forward two or three times to allow all their passengers to alight on the short village platform. There they were invariably met by Military Police of the School Battalion who had purchased large quantities of fish and chips wrapped in newspaper from the nearby shop to resell to the hungry and travel weary GIs at a handsome profit to themselves.

70th ANNIVERSARY

THIS anniversary was marked by a weekend event at Woolacombe combining static exhibitions by living history groups representing units that had attended the Assault Training Centre, spectacular re-creations of beach assaults, vehicle convoys and a wreath laying ceremony.

Woolacombe 70th anniversary event.

Woolacombe 70th anniversary event - beach assault.

Woolacombe 70th anniversary event - beach assault.

Woolacombe 70th anniversary event - beach assault.

Woolacombe 70th anniversary event.

It was the culmination of a year-long project telling schoolchildren of their local wartime heritage and the American "occupation" of North Devon during World War II.

APPENDIX 1

LCVP – Landing Craft Vehicle, Personnel

Of wooden construction with ¼ inch armouring to the ramp and sides it measured 36 feet long, with 10 feet 9 inches beam and a displacement of 17,850 lbs with only a 26 inch draft for a designed load of 30 troops or 2 jeeps.

Alternative engines of a Hall & Scott 250 hp petrol or a Gray 225 bhp diesel gave a range of 102 miles at a speed of 9 knots. The steering position was inside the cargo well, and could be armed with two .30 inch calibre machine guns mounted aft. Between 1942 and 1945, 23,358 were built, the LCVP being the refined and ultimate version of the LCP(R) to the LCV to the LCVP.

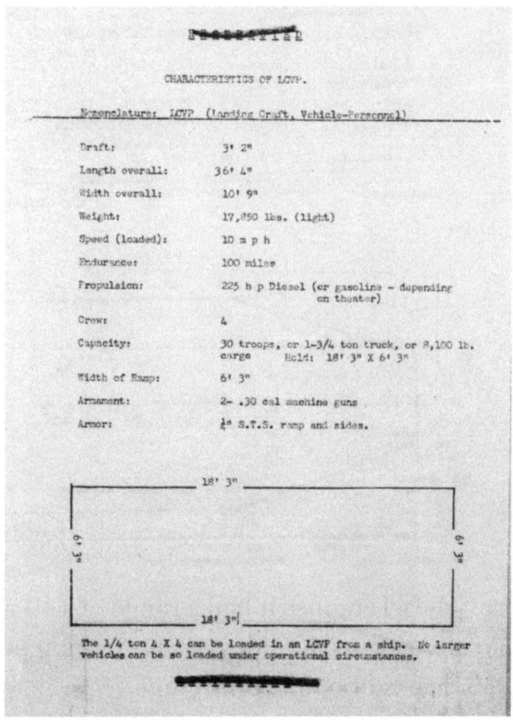

[redacted]

CHARACTERISTICS OF LCVP.

Nomenclature: LCVP (Landing Craft, Vehicle-Personnel)

Draft:	3' 2"
Length overall:	36' 4"
Width overall:	10' 9"
Weight:	17,850 lbs. (light)
Speed (loaded):	10 m p h
Endurance:	100 miles
Propulsion:	225 h p Diesel (or gasoline - depending on theater)
Crew:	4
Capacity:	30 troops, or 1-3/4 ton truck, or 8,100 lb. cargo Hold: 18' 3" X 6' 3"
Width of Ramp:	6' 3"
Armament:	2- .30 cal machine guns
Armor:	¼" S.T.S. ramp and sides.

The 1/4 ton 4 X 4 can be loaded in an LCVP from a ship. No larger vehicles can be so loaded under operational circumstances.

[redacted]

LCM – Landing Craft Mechanised

Of all steel welded construction, 50 feet long with beam of 14 feet in the Mk III version, its designed load was for one 30 ton tank or 60 troops. Powered by

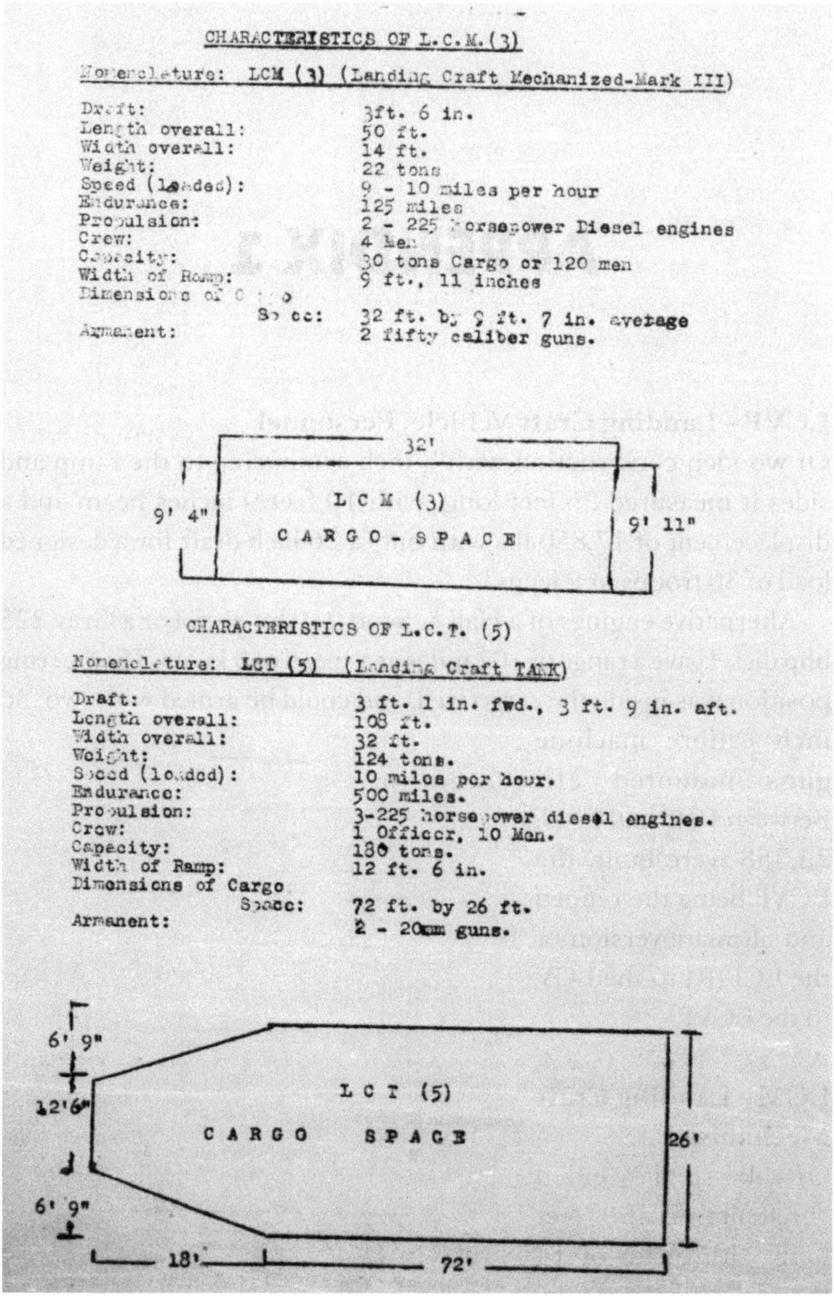

CHARACTERISTICS OF L.C.M.(3)

Nomenclature: LCM (3) (Landing Craft Mechanized-Mark III)

Draft:	3ft. 6 in.
Length overall:	50 ft.
Width overall:	14 ft.
Weight:	22 tons
Speed (loaded):	9 - 10 miles per hour
Endurance:	125 miles
Propulsion:	2 - 225 horsepower Diesel engines
Crew:	4 Men
Capacity:	30 tons Cargo or 120 men
Width of Ramp:	9 ft., 11 inches
Dimensions of Cargo Space:	32 ft. by 9 ft. 7 in. average
Armament:	2 fifty caliber guns.

CHARACTERISTICS OF L.C.T. (5)

Nomenclature: LCT (5) (Landing Craft TANK)

Draft:	3 ft. 1 in. fwd., 3 ft. 9 in. aft.
Length overall:	108 ft.
Width overall:	32 ft.
Weight:	124 tons.
Speed (loaded):	10 miles per hour.
Endurance:	500 miles.
Propulsion:	3-225 horsepower diesel engines.
Crew:	1 Officer, 10 Men.
Capacity:	180 tons.
Width of Ramp:	12 ft. 6 in.
Dimensions of Cargo Space:	72 ft. by 26 ft.
Armament:	2 - 20mm guns.

two diesel engines it had a range of 140 miles at a speed of 11 knots. Armouring to the sides of the steering position and armed with two .50 inch calibre machine guns.

APPENDIX 2

O.S. MAP REF	AREA	ATC	DESCRIPTION
44592-34632	C		Rubble & scree
44602-34396	B		Metal observation tower
44607-36247	D		Beach marker
44622-35106	C	49	Face
44627-36224	D		Beach marker - triangle
44630-34398	B		Beach marker - triangle
44650-36407	D	41	Rubble
44651-35387	C		Scaffold pole (beach marker ?)
44658-36402	D	41	Rubble
44658-34211	B		Pillbox
44663-35099	C		Large concrete blocks
44660-35615	D	46	
44663-35776	D		Sleepers+iron pegs
44665-34206	B		Pillbox walls
44665-35323	C	50	Large remnants + steel
44667-35311	C	48	Face
44660-35615	C	46	Face
44676-35631	C		Face
44684-35459	C	47	Face
44693-35905	D		MoD post
44697-36420	D		Beach marker - triangle
44705-36211	D	43	Remnants + large block
44717-36241	D		Beach marker
44719-36191	D	43	Concrete blocks+steel rods
44721-35814	D	45	Remnants + scree
44724-36188	D		Collapsed pillbox+hessian sacks
44725-34753	C		Large concrete debri
44739-34779	C		Large remnants + steel
44740-35884	D		MoD post

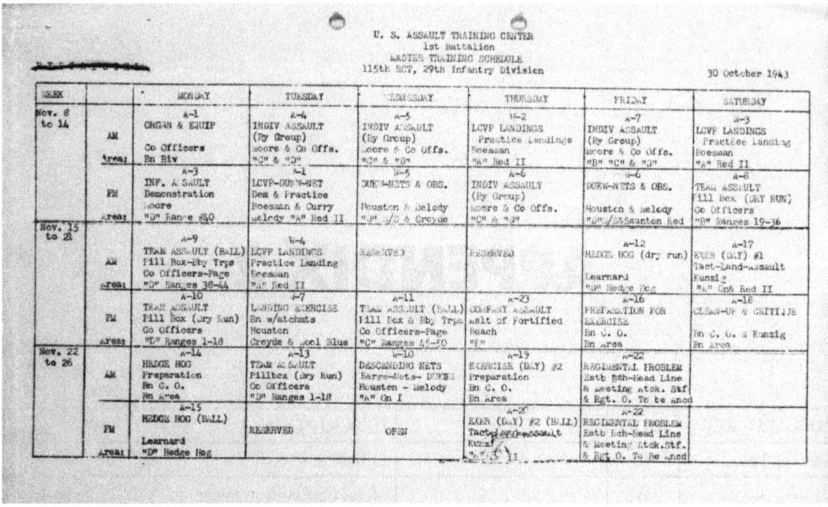

[redacted]

U. S. ASSAULT TRAINING CENTER
1st Battalion
MASTER TRAINING SCHEDULE
115th RCT, 29th Infantry Division

30 October 1943

WEEK		MONDAY	TUESDAY	WEDNESDAY	THURSDAY	FRIDAY	SATURDAY
Nov. 8 to 14	AM Area:	A-1 ORGAN & EQUIP Co Officers Bn Biv	A-4 INDIV ASSAULT (By Group) Moore & Co Offs. "C" & "D"	A-5 INDIV ASSAULT (By Group) Moore & Co Offs. "C" & "D"	W-2 LCVP LANDINGS Practice Landings Boesman "A" Red II	A-7 INDIV ASSAULT (By Group) Moore & Co Offs. "B" "C" & "D"	W-3 LCVP LANDINGS Practice Landing Boesman "A" Red II
	PM Area:	A-3 INF. ASSAULT Demonstration Moore "D" Range #40	W-1 LCVP-DUKW-NET Dem & Practice Boesman & Curry Melody "A" Red II	W-5 DUKW-NETS & OBS. Houston & Melody "D" S/S & Croyde	A-6 INDIV ASSAULT (By Group) Moore & Co Offs. "C" & "D"	W-6 DUKW-NETS & OBS. Houston & Melody "D"S/S&Saunton Red	A-8 TEAM ASSAULT Pill Box (DRY RUN) Co Officers "B" Ranges 19-36
Nov. 15 to 21	AM Area:	A-9 TEAM ASSAULT (BALL) Pill Box-Bby Trps Co Officers-Page "D" Ranges 38-44	W-4 LCVP LANDINGS Practice Landing Boesman "A" Red II	RESERVED	RESERVED	A-12 HEDGE HOG (dry run) Learnard "D" Hedge Hog	A-17 EXER (DAY) #1 Tact-Land-Assault Kunzig "A" Gn& Red II
	PM Area:	A-10 TEAM ASSAULT Pill Box (Dry Run) Co Officers "D" Ranges 1-18	W-7 LANDING EXERCISE Bn w/atchmts Houston Croyde & Pool Blue	A-11 TEAM ASSAULT (BALL) Pill Box & Bby Trps Co Officers-Page "C" Ranges 45-50	A-23 COMPANY ASSAULT Aslt of Fortified Beach "F"	A-16 PREPARATION FOR EXERCISE Bn C. O. Bn Area	A-18 CLEAN-UP & CRITIQUE Bn C. O. & Kunzig Bn Area
Nov. 22 to 26	AM	A-14 HEDGE HOG Preparation Bn C. O. Bn Area	A-13 TEAM ASSAULT Pillbox (Dry Run) Co Officers "D" Ranges 1-18	W-10 DESCENDING NETS Barge-Nets- DUKWS Housten - Melody "A" Gn I	A-19 EXERCISE (DAY) #2 Preparation Bn C. O. Bn Area	A-22 REGIMENTAL PROBLEM Estb Bch-Head Line & Meeting Atck. Stf & Rgt. O. To be Anod	
	PM Area:	A-15 HEDGE HOG (BALL) Learnard "D" Hedge Hog	RESERVED	OPEN	A-20 EXER (DAY) #2 (BALL) Tact-Land-Assault Kunzig [illegible] II	A-22 REGIMENTAL PROBLEM Estb Bch-Head Line & Meeting Atck.Stf. & Rgt O. To Be Anod	

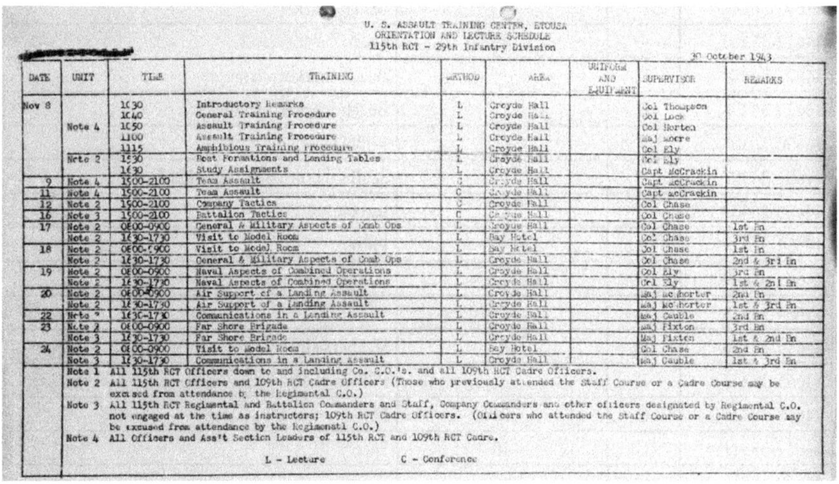

[redacted]

U. S. ASSAULT TRAINING CENTER, ETOUSA
ORIENTATION AND LECTURE SCHEDULE
115th RCT - 29th Infantry Division

30 October 1943

DATE	UNIT	TIME	TRAINING	METHOD	AREA	UNIFORM AND EQUIPMENT	SUPERVISOR	REMARKS
Nov 8	Note 4	1030	Introductory Remarks	L	Croyde Hall		Col Thompson	
		1040	General Training Procedure	L	Croyde Hall		Col Lock	
		1050	Assault Training Procedure	L	Croyde Hall		Col Horton	
		1100	Assault Training Procedure	L	Croyde Hall		Maj Moore	
		1115	Amphibious Training Procedure	L	Croyde Hall		Col Ely	
	Note 2	1530	Boat Formations and Landing Tables	L	Croyde Hall		Col Ely	
		1630	Study Assignments	L	Croyde Hall		Capt McCrackin	
9	Note 4	1900-2100	Team Assault	C	Croyde Hall		Capt McCrackin	
11	Note 4	1900-2100	Team Assault	C	Croyde Hall		Capt McCrackin	
12	Note 2	1900-2100	Company Tactics	C	Croyde Hall		Col Chase	
16	Note 3	1900-2100	Battalion Tactics	C	Croyde Hall		Col Chase	
17	Note 2	0800-0900	General & Military Aspects of Comb Ops	L	Croyde Hall		Col Chase	1st Bn
	Note 2	1630-1730	Visit to Model Room	L	Bay Hotel		Col Chase	3rd Bn
18	Note 2	0800-0900	Visit to Model Room	L	Bay Hotel		Col Chase	1st Bn
	Note 2	1630-1730	General & Military Aspects of Comb Ops	L	Croyde Hall		Col Chase	2nd & 3rd Bn
19	Note 2	0800-0900	Naval Aspects of Combined Operations	L	Croyde Hall		Col Ely	3rd Bn
	Note 2	1630-1730	Naval Aspects of Combined Operations	L	Croyde Hall		Col Ely	1st & 2nd Bn
20	Note 2	0800-0900	Air Support of a Landing Assault	L	Croyde Hall		Maj McWhorter	2nd Bn
	Note 2	1630-1730	Air Support of a Landing Assault	L	Croyde Hall		Maj McWhorter	1st & 3rd Bn
22	Note ?	1630-1730	Communications in a Landing Assault	L	Croyde Hall		Maj Cauble	2nd Bn
23	Note 2	0800-0900	Far Shore Brigade	L	Croyde Hall		Maj Fixton	3rd Bn
	Note 3	1630-1730	Far Shore Brigade	L	Croyde Hall		Maj Fixton	1st & 2nd Bn
24	Note 2	0800-0900	Visit to Model Room	L	Bay Hotel		Col Chase	2nd Bn
	Note 3	1630-1730	Communications in a Landing Assault	L	Croyde Hall		Maj Cauble	1st & 3rd Bn

Note 1 All 115th RCT Officers down to and including Co. C.O.'s. and all 109th RCT Cadre Officers.
Note 2 All 115th RCT Officers and 109th RCT Cadre Officers (Those who previously attended the Staff Course or a Cadre Course may be excused from attendance by the Regimental C.O.)
Note 3 All 115th RCT Regimental and Battalion Commanders and Staff, Company Commanders and other officers designated by Regimental C.O. not engaged at the time as instructors; 109th RCT Cadre Officers. (Officers who attended the Staff Course or a Cadre Course may be excused from attendance by the Regimenatl C.O.)
Note 4 All Officers and Ass't Section Leaders of 115th RCT and 109th RCT Cadre.

L - Lecture C - Conference

O.S. MAP REF	AREA	ATC	DESCRIPTION
44754-35981	D	44	Rubble + corrugated shuttering
44762-36911	D		Damaged face
44770-36380	D	42	Estimated
44775-36294	D		BWSP
44777-34736	C	51	
44790-34762	C		Scaffold poles (road edge markers)
44791-34075	B	Engr Obstacle Course	Concrete lump
44792-36295	D		BWSP
44792-36493	D		8 Mounds in pattern
44794-34764	C		Scaffold poles (road edge markers)

APPENDIX 2

[redacted]

U. S. ASSAULT TRAINING CENTER
INFANTRY TRAINING PROGRAM
ASSAULT TRAINING

30 October 1943

Code	Hours	Method	Description of Training	Uniform	Place	Reference	Supervisor
A-1	4	P	Organization	Field	Bn Biv Area	Trng Notes, Inf Aslt Aslt Ch II Trng Memo, Orgn of Aslt Bn Trng Notes, Personal Equip Trng Notes, Signal Comm.	Co Officers
A-3	4	D	Dem of Assault Section	Field	"D" Range 40		Moore
A-4	4		Individual Assault Technique & Tactical Employment of: 1. Flame Thrower *2. Demolition D *3. Rocket *4. Rifle P *5. M. G. & BAR *6. Mortar 7. Wire Cutters *Each Co will send 1 qualified officer to each of these groups and to other groups if they are available. Instruction in rifle, BAR M.G. and Mortar is by Company Officers with Training Center Staff Officers as advisors.	Field	Rifles, Mortars, Machine Guns, BAR report to "D" Range 40 - All others to respective ranges Aslt Gp Tng Assign 1. Flame Thrower Rng "G" 2. Demolition Area "C" Trng Notes, Inf Aslt Ch II 3. Rocket Rng "C" Trng Guides 4. 37-43 incl(less 40 "D") 5. 44 - 46 incl. "C" 6. 48 - 51 incl. "C" 7. "D" So. of Aslt Rgn 16		Moore [illegible] Lewis Co Officers Co Officers Co Officers Hauser
A-5	4	P	Individual Assault Continuation of A-4 (Progressive)	Field	Same as A-4 except report to group ranges.	Trng Notes, Inf Aslt, Ch II; Lesson Plans; Trng Guides	Same as A-4
A-6	4	P	Individual Assault Continuation of A-4 (Progressive)	Field	Same as A-5	Trng Notes, Inf Aslt, Ch II - Lesson Plans	Same as A-4
A-7	4	P	Individual Assault Continuation of A-4 (Progressive)	Field	Same as A-5 except Rifle-Zen to 19-24 incl Area E	Trng Notes, Inf Aslt Ch II, Lesson Plans	Same as A-4
A-8	4	P	Team Assault Assault of Pill Box (Dry Run)	Field	"E" Rng 19-36 incl. "D" Rng 1 - 18 incl.	Trng Notes, Inf Aslt ChI; Trng Memo, Coord of Tms & Aslt Sections Lesson Plans Trng Guides	Co Officers

[redacted]

INFANTRY PROGRAM, ASSAULT TRAINING (Cont'd)

30 October 1943

Code	Hours	Method	Description of Training	Uniform	Place	References	Supervisor
A-9	2 2	P	Team Assault Assault of Pill Box (Ball Am) 1 hr each to booby traps #1 & 2 or 3 & 4	Field	"C" Rng 45-50 incl "D" 38-44 incl	Same as A-8	Co Officers Page
A-10	4	P	Team Assault Assault of Pill Box (Dry Run)	Field	"E" Rngs 19-36 incl "D" Rngs 1 - 18 incl	Same as A-8	Co Officers
A-11	2 2	P P	Team Assault Assault of Pill Box (Ball Am) 1 hr each to booby traps #3 & 4 or #1 & 2	Field	"D" Rngs 38-44 incl "C" Rng 45-50 incl	Same as A-8	Co Officers Page
A-12	4	D&P	Dry Run Aslt of Hedge-Hog (to perfect details of technique & timing in preparation for A-15)	Field	"D" Hedge-Hog		Learnard
A-13	4	P	Assault of Pill Box (Dry Run)	Field	("D" Rngs 1-18 incl) ("E" Rngs 19-36 incl)	Same as A-8	Co Officers
A-14	4	P	Preparation for Exercise	Field	Bn Area	Exercise Hedge-Hog	Bn.CO
A-15	4	Ex	Exercise Hedge-Hog (Ball Am)	Field	"D" Hedge-Hog	Exercise Hedge-Hog	Learnard
A-16	4	P	Preparation for Exercise	Field	Bn Area	Field Exercise #3	Bn C. O.
A-17	4	Ex	Tactical Landing Assault	Field, Life Belts	"A" Esty Gn II & Red II Woolacombe	Field Exercise #3	Kunzig
A-18	4	P	Critique and Cleanup after exercise	Field	Bn Biv Area		Kunzig & Bn CO
A-19	4	P	Preparation for Exercise	Field	Bn Area	Field Exercise #3	Bn C. O.
A-20	4	Ex	Tactical Landing Assault (Ball AM)	Field Life Belts	"A" Esty Gn II & Red II Woolacombe	Field Exercise #3	Kunzig & Bn C. O.
A-21	4	P	Critique & Cleanup after Exercise	Field	Bn Biv Area		Kunzig & Bn CO
A-22	8	Ex	Regimental Problem: Est. of Beach Head Line & Meeting Counter-attack	Field Life Belts	To Be Announced		Kunzig & Regt C. O.
A-23	4	P	Company Assault Assault of Fortified Beach by Company	Field	Area "F" (Baggy Point)		Co. C. O.

NOTE: When more than one location is given, see schedule for location of a particular period.

[redacted]

U. S. ASSAULT TRAINING CENTER
INFANTRY TRAINING PROGRAM
AMPHIBIOUS TRAINING

30 October 1943

Code	Hour	Method	Description of Training	Uniform	Place	Reference	Supervisor
W-1	1	D	(1) LCVP Demonstration & Lecture - Embarkation & Debarkation	Field & Belts	"A" Red II	Trng Memo. "Dbkn in a ship to shore operation"	Maj Boesman
	1½	P	(2) LCVP Mock-Up practice	"	"A" LCVP Mock-up Area	Trng Memo "Embktn into & Dbkn from LC"	Co Officers
	1	D&P	(3) DUKW Demonstration & Practice	"	"A" Blue I		Capt Curry
	½	D	(4) Net Debarkation Demonstration	"	"A" Yellow II		Capt Melody
W-2	4	P	LCVP Landing - Practice Landing. Embark on beaches Red II & Green II. Land on Yellow 1. March to Red II repeat	"	"A" Red II	Training Guide	Maj Boesman
W-3	4	P	LCVP Landing - Practice Landings. Embark on beaches Red II & Green II. Land on beach Croyde Yellow, weather permitting. Alternate, land on beach Green I, march to embkn behs. Rpt	"	" " "	" "	" "
W-4	(Same as W-3)						
*W-5	2	P	First half battalion mount in DUKW's. Carried to Croyde or Saunton Red Beach. Voyage. Land, reassemble. Return to S/S in DUKW's.	"	"D" Ship sides	" "	Lt Col Houston & Capt Melody
*W-5	2	P	First half Battalion: Nets & Obstacles.	"	"D" S/S	" "	"
*W-5	2	P	Second half Battalion: Nets & Obstacles	"	" "	" "	"
*W-5	2	P	Second half Battalion: Mount in DUKW.	"	" "	" "	"
*W-6	(Same as W-5)						
*W-7	4	P	Landing exercise. Bn with attachments in DUKW'S. Bn less Vehicular units, embark at Croyde Yellow & Woolacombe Blue. Land at Woolacombe Green. Controlled advance. Vehicular units fed in from other parts of beach.	"	Croyde & Woolacombe Blue		Lt Col Houston
*W-8	(Same as W-5)						
*W-9	(Same as W-5)						
*W-10	2 2 4	P P P	First half Battalion. Individual Trng embarking in DUKW's or LCVP, transfer to barge, ascend net into floating boat or DUKW, return to beach. repeat. Tactical Landing in DUKW'S. Second half Bn. Tactical DUKW Landing.(2hrs) Nets on Barge (2 hrs)	"	"A" Green 1		Capt Melody

*On account of uncertainties of weather, five periods primarily involving DUKWS have been scheduled. The first three periods permitted by weather will be used. DUKW periods cancelled on account of weather, or DUKW periods remaining after three have been covered, will be released to Bn Commanders, with notification as far ahead as is made practicable by weather forecast. Other training facilities will be made available to the Bn Commander.

O.S. MAP REF	AREA	ATC	DESCRIPTION
44825-34960	C		Many collapsed pits+concrete
44810-36940	D	39	Estimated
44819-33962	B		MoD post
44834-34168	B	Engr Obstacle Course	Concrete debri
44835-36730	D	40	Estimated
44836-34163	B		Surface debri
44843-34810	C		Road section
44837-34160	B	Engr Obstacle Course	Reinforcing steel rod
44838-36838	D	12	Estimated
44841-34149	B	Engr Obstacle Course	Scattered concrete debri
44844-34153	B	Engr Obstacle Course	Scattered concrete debri
44844-34155	B	Engr Obstacle Course	Scattered concrete debri
44890-36213	D		MoD post
44891-35414	C		Concrete post
44905-36325	D	13	Estimated
44946-36808	D		Concrete blocks in heap
44951-35954	D	15	BWSP
44953-36290	D	14	BWSP to 250503/GK
44964-35944	D		BWSP
44965-33509	B	19	No trace
44965-36560	D	11	Steel reinforcing rods+BWSP
44972-35935	D		BWSP
44973-36124	D		BWSP
44980-36510	D		North-south line humps (9)
44985-36439	D		9 Humps
44988-35930	D		Wire
44988-35932	D		Tank shell head
44988-36237	D		Concrete debri + stone
44990-34500	C	Rocket Range	Wall
44990-36167	D		Ridge to 45062-36193
44997-36255	D		BWSP
44998-36184	D		BWSPs
45000-32580	A		Many bases - blown
45001-36246	D		BWSP
45002-35826	D		Formed concrete debri
45004-36239	D		BWSP
45007-33259	B	21	Face - rubble - over large area
45008-36225	D		BWSP from 250503/GG
45015-33420	B	20	Mound
45021-36062	D		BWSPs
45027-36509	D		Surface debri

O.S. MAP REF	AREA	ATC	DESCRIPTION
45029-33274	B		Concrete surface rubble
45037-33243	B		Pillbox shattered
45039-36443	D		Shrapnel
45044-36329	D		Concrete debri & Tank
45045-36830	D	10	Estimated
45061-36071	D		Many BWSPs (possible dump)
45069-36324	D		Tank+concrete surface debri
45077-36423	D		Shrapnel+BWSP+mortars
45100-36920	D	6	Estimated
45140-36400	D	7H	Estimated
45146-37035	D		Standing walls & large debri
45155-36330	D	12H	Estimated
45165-33878	B	Dragons teeth	Large remnants + steel
45166-33964	B	Engr Demo Range	Angle iron+wire in parallel lines
45180-36298	D		Many mounds
45185-36381	D	7H	Metal debri+shapes
45187-33545	B		Scattered remnants
45189-35412	C		Scree+shrapnel+wire
45197-34105	B	Engr Demo Range	extends eastwards
45200-35323	C		Metal tube+corrugated
45203-33580	B		Remnants+post holes
45203-33378	B		BWSP
45207-35323	C		Concrete slabs+timbers
45209-36188	D		BWSP
45210-36420	D	6H	Estimated
45211-33999	B	Engr Demo Range	Angle iron+rail length
45216-33960	B	Engr Demo Range	Concrete post+rail length
45226-33621			Causeway border marker
45228-33398	B	52	Crater+remnants+BWSP
45228-33041	B	23	Scattered remnants
45232-35288	C		Mound+rubble+sawn timbers
45234-33597	B		concrete post bases
45235-33368	B		BWSP
45235-33062	B		Large concrete debri & steel
45236-33590	B		15xpost bases - edge markers ?
45236-33649			Causeway border marker
45237-35947	D		Sleepers
45238-33610			Causeway border marker
45240-33597			Causeway border marker
45240-36550	D	5H	Estimated
45241-33585			Causeway border marker

O.S. MAP REF	AREA	ATC	DESCRIPTION
45244-34233	B	Engr Demo Range	to 45270-34211
45246-34179	B	Engr Demo Range	to 45225-34187
45248-34333	B	Engr Demo Range	to 45279-34326
45250-34353	B	Engr Demo Range	to 45273-34347
45250-36190	D	9H	Estimated
45253-33578			Causeway border marker
45353-33583			Causeway border marker
45253-33593			Causeway border marker
45255-33575			Causeway border marker
45256-34252	B	Engr Demo Range	to 45228-34263
45258-34306	B	Engr Demo Range	Scaffold+angle iron+wire
45266-34152	B	Engr Demo Range	Metal corrugated zig-zag
45269-33612	B		Remnants
45271-34298	B	Engr Demo Range	Scaffold+angle iron+wire
45272-33614	B		Remnants
45273-35864	D		Shrapnel
45277-33188	B		BWSP
45284-33239	B		Concrete debri
45286-33491	B		MoD post
45287-33236	B		Large concrete remnants
45294-36220	D		Ridge to 45324-36332
45295-33002	B	24	Remnants - small
45303-34293	B	Engr Demo Range	to 45298-34293
45306-33458	B	26	Concrete surface debri
45320-36260	D	8H	Estimated
45323-36528	D		BWSP + mortar rounds
45325-33340	B	25	Estimated
45338-33042	B		Remnants scattered
45345-33276	B	22	Mound
45356-35864	D		Post
45389-36350	D	Hedgehog	N-S ridge - from here
45390-35870	D		Post
45407-36531	D		Several BWSPs
45407-36552	D		Wire
45410-36185	D	10H	Estimated
45412-36540	D		BWSPs
45435-36502	D	Hedgehog	N-S ridge - to here
45444-35878	D		Post
45450-36050	D	1H	Estimated
45475-36910	D	7	Estimated
45482-33668	B		2 x concrete post bases

O.S. MAP REF	AREA	ATC	DESCRIPTION
45495-36300	D	2H	Estimated
45500-36450	D	11H	Estimated
45512-32837	B	36	Surface rubble+cement+bitumen
45517-33014	B		Remnants - small
45538-32993	B	31	Remnants - small
45555-35940	D	16	Estimated
45562-32693	B		Pillbox - debri
45570-36350	D	3H	Estimated
45570-36710	D	8	Estimated
45580-36520	D	4H	Estimated
45582-35768	D	17	Concrete slabs+timbers
4558-3459	C	Unidentified	Mound & wall
45586-32720	B		MoD post
45594-32741	B		MoD post
45605-35710	D		Bunker destroyed+collapsed wall
45610-35693	D		Concrete wall collapsed
45612-33372	B		Metal tanks - flamethrower
45650-35750	D		ruin
45745-33021	B		Concrete surface debri
45760-36550	D	9	Estimated
45774-33325	B	28	Concrete+hedge+ditch
45775-33507	B	27	Large debri (Pillbox)
45776-33027	B		Concrete surface rubble
45777-33317	B	29	Large debri
45777-34380	B		Roadtrack+heap overgrown
45792-33493	B		Scattered concrete debri
45804-32640	B	Assembly area	Concrete base
45815-33045	B	32	Surface concrete rubble
45820-32627	A	Assembly area	Single concrete base
45820-33505	B		Road wire+2" mortars
45825-32662	B		Two upright timber planks
45885-32630	B	35	Estimated
45918-32861	B		Single concrete lump
45925-32660	B	34	Estimated
45933-35337	C		Single concrete lump
45936-32911	B		Surface rubble+steel rods
45957-32917	B	Unidentified	Large remnants+steel(Pillbox)
45950-32927	B	33	
45990-33795	B	Unidentified	Concrete base 6ftx6ft
46003-32560	B		Many bases - blown
46046-32656	B		Concrete base

O.S. MAP REF	AREA	ATC	DESCRIPTION
46080-33254	B	30	Single reinforcing bar
46095-33190	B		LCT mockup
46119-35247	D		"Mortuary"
46122-33180	B		LCT mockup + plaque
46137-33146	B		LCT mockup
46166-33080	B		LCT mockup
46206-33082	A		LCT mockup
46208-35722	D		Concrete construction spoil
46230-32627	A		1940 .303 cartridge
4625-3585	D	Unidentified	bases within treeline
46275-33120	A		LCM base
46293-33125	B		LCM base
46303-33332	A		Surface debri
46321-33055	A		post
46335-33093	A		LCM base
46348-33114	B		Debri - probably LCM base

APPENDIX 3

4. Steel Obstacles

Obstacle	Description	Hand-placed charge	Placement	Minimum Safety Distance	Sketch
a. Rail obstacle (Timber post obstacle similar)	(1) R.R. sharpened, driven in upright or at 45° angle. (2) Bent Rail	1 block C-2 per footing	At foot of rail. Connect charges w/primacord. Charge in close contact with rail.	50 yds	
b. Steel Scaffolding.	2" Pipe barrier, with friction joints, made into frame 9' high.	Bangalore Torpedoes 10 lengths.	Tied to vertical and sloping main members.	100 yds	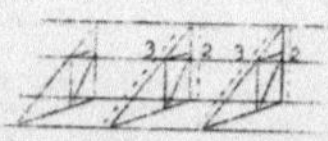
c. Tetrahedrons	5 ft on a side; made of 6" steel members.	2 blocks C-2	Placed at all four corners. (1/2 block per corner)	50 yds	
d. HedgeHog	Three 6" x 6" steel members welded at center or with block of concrete cast at center.	1 block C-2	At center of cross. Close contact	50 yds	
e. Chevaux-de-Frise	Made of 2" steel tubing, covered with wire.	One length of bangalore.	Along main member.	30 yds (on axis of bangalore)	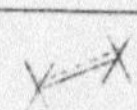

(Continued on Page 4)

- 3 -

3. Concrete Obstacles

Obstacle	Description	Hand-placed charge	Placement	Minimum Safety Distance	Sketch
a. Reinforced Concrete Wall	10' high 8' thick	(1) Approximately 2 lbs C-2/ft^3 of gap desired.	Outline gap in U-shape w/3/4 of charge; place 1/4 in center.	100 yds	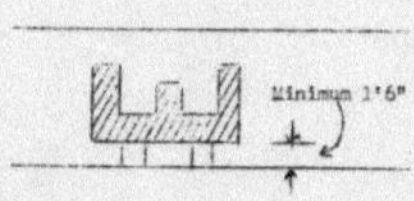
b. R.C. cube, cylinder, or egg.	4' x 4' x 4'	2 packs C-2	On ground, on side.	50 yds	
c. R.C. coffin	3' x 3' x 5'	1 pack C-2	On ground midway of long side, against coffin.	50 yds	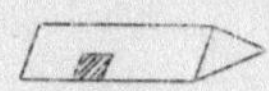
d. R.C. Dragon's Teeth	6' high 3' high 2' high	(a) For individual teeth: 2 packs C-2 ½ pack C-2 ¼ pack C-2 (b) If base is above ground, see atchd Sketch "B"	On ground beside (a) tooth or (b) base	100 yds	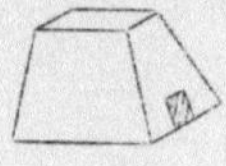

- 2 -

4. Steel Obstacles (Continued)

Obstacle	Description	Hand-placed charge	Placement	Minimum Safety Distance	Sketch
f. Element "C"	Structural steel gate.	C-2 blocks at specified joints.	Place charges to cut all vertical members at top and bottom	50 yds	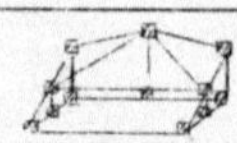
g. Curved Rail	Structural steel rails.	Same	Same	50 yds	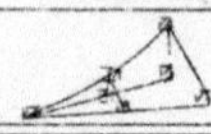
5. Ditch Obstacles					
a. Triangular ditch.	Triangular cross-section	3 C-2 packs	Charges placed along ditch, on parapet.	25 yds	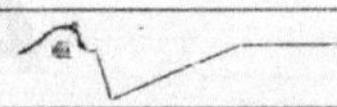
b. Trapezoidal ditch		6 C-2 packs	Same, but placed on both sides of ditch	25 yds	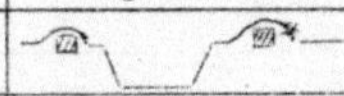
c. Ditch revetted with concrete, up to 1 ft thick.	Either cross-section	C-2 packs side by side across gap width.	On parapet or against revetted wall, 1/3 way up	50 yds	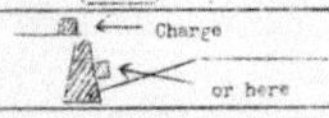
d. Covered ditch	Normal ditch with brick or wooden cover	Same. Use wall-breaching data if concrete revetments over 1 ft thick.	Same, except for heavy concrete revetment.	100 yds	

"I said it's to give you guys a little idea of what the real thing's like!"

And he isn't kidding!!

#0007 - 190418 - C0 - 229/152/8 - PB - 9781908336668